Letters to the Precious Group

By Lucy Blount

Illustrated by Mary Barwick

Library of Congress Catalog No. 91-090462
ISBN 0-9630017-0-1

Light-bearers Publishers, Inc.
P.O. Box 348
Montgomery, Alabama 36101-0348
205-265-5601
205-834-8406 FAX

Editors: Mots Rainer and Jean Waters, Montgomery, Alabama
Designer: Toffaletti Design, Montgomery, Alabama
Printer: Craftsman Printing, Inc., Birmingham, Alabama

Cover:
Jump Rope With A Rainbow,
by Mary Barwick

Letters to the Precious Group

In Memory Of
Dexter Cummings Hobbs
September 4, 1955 – April 22, 1990

Thank you, Father Bill Russell, for the quiet smiles of encouragement.
Thank you, Mary Barwick, for the hugs of joy and for knowing that "ah ha's" are real.
Thank you, family and friends for never doubting the outcome.
Thank you, Jean Waters, for your enthusiasm from day one and your grammatical skills.
Thank you, Mark Waldo and Carl Bear, Jr., for helpful critiques.
Thank you, OV members, for the weekly encouragement and prayers.
Thank you, Bill McMillan, for sharing your wisdom and your
declaration of, "Don't give up, Lucy."
Thank you, Mots Rainer, Julie Toffaletti, and Pearlie Prad, for turning
the manuscript into a book, the dream into a reality.
Thank you, Winton, for pleasantly proofreading and
putting up with me during this birthing.
And lastly, but most importantly, I thank my Heavenly Father
for allowing me the privilege of writing these
letters to the "Precious Group."
May they be to His glory!
Love, Lucy

Dedicated to the original "Precious Group," my children,
Winton, Stuart, Will and Jud. And of course, to my precious husband, Winton –
ILY and ITGFY.
Lucy

Dedicated to love, laughter and a sense of wonder in God's great tapestry.
Mary

Contents

Precious Group, Let's Go Deeper

Precious Group, Let's Go Lighter

Illustrations

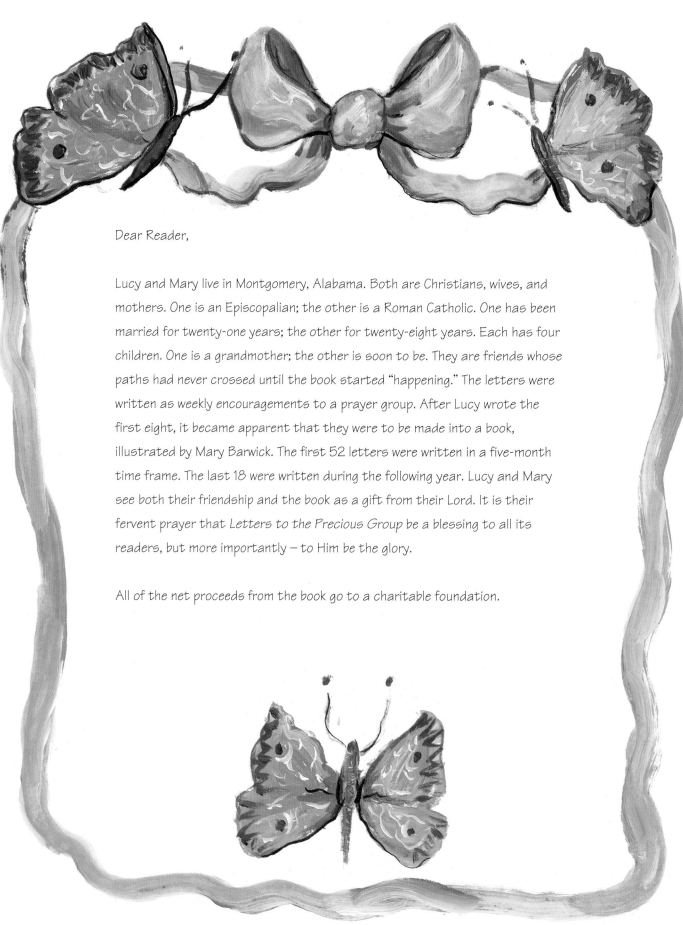

Dear Reader,

Lucy and Mary live in Montgomery, Alabama. Both are Christians, wives, and mothers. One is an Episcopalian; the other is a Roman Catholic. One has been married for twenty-one years; the other for twenty-eight years. Each has four children. One is a grandmother; the other is soon to be. They are friends whose paths had never crossed until the book started "happening." The letters were written as weekly encouragements to a prayer group. After Lucy wrote the first eight, it became apparent that they were to be made into a book, illustrated by Mary Barwick. The first 52 letters were written in a five-month time frame. The last 18 were written during the following year. Lucy and Mary see both their friendship and the book as a gift from their Lord. It is their fervent prayer that *Letters to the Precious Group* be a blessing to all its readers, but more importantly – to Him be the glory.

All of the net proceeds from the book go to a charitable foundation.

Precious Group,

I love C.S. Lewis – some of his images set my heart on fire, allowing me to comprehend a little deeper some of God's truths. One such image that I've cherished is his "Bent People" – his idea being, we're all bent – we're all sinners.

This helps me stop judging people. Instead of "minus 10, she's a glutton," and then, "Oh, there goes a minus 40," and look at that "minus 80, I better not get too close!" Boy, I could really work myself up to a sinful "minus 100" – false pride, in that mindset. The "Bent People" help me to break away from that horrid judging of others, but I need to go further – I think we all need to go further.

Luke 13:10-13: "And He was teaching in one of the synagogues on the Sabbath, and behold, there was a woman who for 18 years had had a sickness caused by a spirit; and she was bent double and could not straighten up at all. And when Jesus saw her, He called her over and said to her, 'Woman, you are freed from your sickness.' And he laid hands upon her and immediately she was made erect again and began glorifying God."

As redeemed sinners, washed in the blood of the Lamb, we no longer have curvature of the spine. Stand tall and praise Him!

Your sister in Christ,

Lucy

Precious Group,

"Come Thou Long Expected Jesus, Born to Set Thy People Free" – Advent – getting ready for the King to come – thrilling.

Yesterday I woke up at 5:00 a.m. We had a football party the day before at the lake. Needless to say, there was plenty to clean up. I didn't want to awaken anyone, so I crept down the stairs in the dark to clean up the mess and there was one!

As I washed the dishes I thought, I've got to finish before sunrise – for I wanted to go up to the top of our house and watch. Well, it was as exciting as waiting for Santa to come on Christmas Eve. By the time I finished, the sky was a pale gray.

I quietly crept upstairs and had a full 20 minutes waiting – gosh, it went slowly! The light seemed like it took forever to come. From gray, to a little brighter, so I could see the wind was really blowing white caps on the water and birds and trees were actively moving. I felt like we were all getting ready – very exciting!

It was a slow birthing. Each moment the sky seemed to take on another color. There were more shades of blue, pink and gold. And then it showed its glorious face. Well, you couldn't help but burst out and say, "This is the day that the Lord hath made. We will rejoice and be glad in it!"

We are all living in an "advent" season – our whole lives – the King is coming! Walk in that knowledge with excitement and anticipation. Get ready with the same enthusiasm as a child on Christmas Eve! It is a privilege to get our "temples" in order – for He is coming! Hallelujah!

Your sister in Christ,

Lucy

Dec. 16

Precious Group,

"Come Thou Long Expected Jesus, Born to Set Thy People Free!" Yea! I'm at the lake again and when I woke up 15 minutes ago, that was the song in my heart. I'm curled up on the sofa with a down comforter, drinking Swiss Mocha – watching you know what again!

It's different watching the sunrise on the first floor than on the 3rd floor. The Lord's glorious sunrise – is that – it's again glorious – but my perspective has changed! I'm not sitting with my head in the clouds, feeling like I'm soaring with the birds, but on ground level. I can almost touch the steel gray lake – it's flowing so fast, about as fast as I feel that I've been going the last week – not even aware of the daily sunrises. There are little puffs of vapor dancing here and there over the water and then evaporating. It's really as beautiful as the golden sky that's taking place, in a cold, austere, gray type of way. Gosh, that sounds like "Doom and Gloom!"

Guess what just happened? It has risen! It's up! And guess what's happening to the water? It's shining, with pink reflections – beautiful! For me the water represents us and our fast-paced world; the dancing mist = Holy Spirit; the glorious sun = our Heavenly Father, and thanks be to the Dear Lord – Jesus walked on water! He knows our world and its pressures. He has empathy and understanding. He's been here – and He's coming again!

John 6:17b: "It had become dark and Jesus had not yet come to them, and the sea began to be stirred up because a strong wind was blowing. When therefore, they had rowed about three or four miles, they beheld Jesus walking on the sea and drawing near to the boat; and they were frightened. But He said to them, "It is I; do not be afraid."

Can you relate? Have you been rowing about three or four miles out this past week, rowing as fast as you can, really getting nowhere, but tired and forgetting the most important passenger – who calms storms, takes fears away, turns a gray, steel world into pink?

"Come Thou Long Expected Jesus, Born to Set Thy People Free" – He is here! He wants to give you freedom – allow Him to this advent, so that you can be shot with glory.

The lake's blue now, as blue as the sky. With a little of the right exposure, it's reflecting the glorious sky. Could it be the same for us with just a little bit of the right exposure?

"Come Thou Long Expected Jesus…."

Your sister in Christ,

Lucy

Precious Group,

I'm hiding! Shhh! Don't tell! My goal today was to write you two letters, for our family's going to be gone for a week skiing and we'll be out of touch – physically, but not spiritually! Well, I was successful in writing the first one as everything was quiet and beautiful and undisturbed. You see, I have a one-track mind and I really have to focus, with no distractions, to write. Well, as soon as I finished the first letter real life invaded – precious Winton. At 7:00 a.m. the stereo's blasting – the doors opened (freezing) to go get the wood to start a fire – the newspaper's being read out loud to me – then going to the store for coffee – then shower-ing – then – well "Good Morning, Vietnam" – a real day has begun. Jud wakes up so now I have two precious men wanting attention. (But I want to write a letter!)

One more time I say with great confidence, "Winton, why don't you fix breakfast?" (This is not the usual Saturday morning scenario in our twenty years of marriage, but I'm an optimist!) "And Jud, you go study for your history exam." (Again, an optimist.) "I'll clean up the dishes."

I run, yes run, upstairs to the second floor, thinking, now's my chance! Winton has a wonderful office tower room on the second floor. It's two stories – one wall is all windows and the opposite wall is a stairway leading to the Chaplet – a diminutive chapel (named by a precious elderly Sunday School teacher). There is a 6' x 4' landscape painting hanging over the door and a beam of light is shining straight down on it from the stairwell. Gosh, I thought, this is just like how the shepherds must have felt that starry night – minding their sheep, business as usual – when glory dropped in.

Luke 2:9: "And in the same region there were some shepherds staying out in the fields and keeping watch over their flock by night. And an angel of the Lord suddenly stood before them; and they were terribly frightened. And the angel said to them, 'Do not be afraid; for today in the city of David there has been born for you a Saviour who is Christ the Lord.'"

I was so excited, "Thank you, Lord," I have something to write about! I quietly sneaked back down the stairs for some tea. My men were playing cards and eating leftover rice and steak. (Oh well! Not the breakfast I planned, but I bet I still will get to do the dishes!) I fixed my tea and crept back upstairs – excited that everything was just right. But the beam was no longer shining. The painting, which is wonderful, was again, just wonderful, but no longer glorious!

What a let-down! What a disappointment! I wanted to look and look and think and ponder and enjoy and dream and pray – but the glory was gone. But maybe it would have been too much. Maybe it would have dulled my senses instead of heightened them – like too much chocolate cake.

Luke 2:13–15: "And suddenly there appeared with the angel a multitude of heavenly host praising God and saying, 'Glory to God in the highest, and on earth peace among men with whom He is pleased.'

And it came about when the angels had gone away from them into heaven, that the shepherds began saying to one another, 'Let us go straight to Bethlehem then and see this thing that has happened which the Lord has made known to us.'"

I bet that invasion of glory lasted only a moment! It would have been the ultimate "laser show" which their finite minds would have tried to comprehend– would have tried to relate to others – but somehow would never have been able to recapture. I bet those shepherds were never the same, for they knew all the way down to their deepest level – that He is!

I'm sure each one of us has had an invasion of glory sometime during his life – the first view of your child, a bird singing, children giggling, a Daddy and a son playing cards and eating steak and rice for breakfast. He is!

Merry Christmas! Let's live in the glory!

Your sister in Christ,
Lucy

Precious Group,

"I will lift up mine eyes unto the hills, from whence cometh my help. My help cometh from the Lord, which made heaven and earth." **Psalm 121:1-2.**

It is Christmas Eve in British Columbia. I'm sitting alone outside on top of the world. Oh, I wish I could capture in words the awesome view. There are gigantic mountain peaks all the way around me. They seem to have broken through the clouds reaching to the sky – reaching to their Creator.

I rode two chair lifts up the mountain to get to this height. When we broke through the clouds and came out into the sunlight, my son's fiancée (a first-time skier) said, "It's just like heaven!" And it was! Then we kept climbing and climbing until the whole world was below the clouds. It was just me, my daughter, and my son's fiancée in total quietness, climbing and climbing, just clouds, mountains, sky, and trees. Awesome – a holy moment.

The Bible tells of Jesus going to the mountains to be alone to pray and to teach. It was to a high mountain that our Lord was transfigured, where He communed with Elijah and Moses. It was on a mountain where He was betrayed. It was on a mountain where He died. It was on a mountain where He ascended to Heaven.

At this moment I can comprehend a little deeper what the psalmist was saying – how somehow mountains capture the incomprehensible strength of our God – our Creator.

At this moment I am profoundly thankful that our Lord Jesus had the visible strength of the mountains and hills to recall to Him the Nature of His Father during many of the trials in His life.

The clouds, wind, sun, trees, skiers are all in motion but the mountains – ah, the mountains are solid as a rock – solid as our Lord God. "Our Lord is our Rock and our Salvation." There are no variables in this! It is His strength on which we rely. We are on solid, victorious ground! Hallelujah!

Dec. 25

Precious Group,

Merry Christmas! I'm back on the mountain again. Today there are no clouds. I can see all the way down into the valley. I found a corner table in the warm-up house. There are windows on two sides. I feel like I'm in a nest on top of a big fir tree, for right outside there are huge trees and I'm at their same height. Perched just like the birds I'm watching, but I'm a lot warmer and cozier. In fact, life doesn't get much better – sipping coffee – listening to classical music – waiting for family – well, my cup runneth over!

The most unbelievable serendipity gift of the day, however, is in the next corner. There is a beautiful mother nursing her baby. Of course, I couldn't resist going to talk to her (my children would have died from embarrassment). The baby's name is Terah and she's two months old and this is her first trip up to the mountains.

Oh, the smile of that mother, the pride, the joy, that universal shine that only a new mother has. I thank the Dear Lord that He allowed me the privilege of seeing this smile on this particular day, once again refreshing my memory of that unique maternal glow. I thank the Dear Lord that we have the "Magnificat." **Luke 1:46-55**. I thank the Dear Lord that it says, "Mary treasured up all these things and pondered them in her heart," **Luke 2:19**, for I believe every mother sings a glorious song of thanksgiving at the miracle of her child's birth – the unfathomable miracle.

Each baby represents hopes and dreams and love. Of course, Jesus came into this fallen world as a baby. What better way could God represent love – except later – by crucifixion.

"For unto us is born this day in the city of David, a Saviour which is Christ the Lord!" **Luke 2:11.** That smile reminds me that He is! Thank you, Lord God! Merry Christmas!

Your sister in Christ,

Lucy

Dec. 31

Precious Group,

It's a gray, dreary day. I'm on my favorite sofa at the lake, which should help, but it doesn't. Everything out the window looks flat and blah. I mean a gray day! There is no fire crackling in the fireplace to make things glow and be cozy, because it is too warm. The trees are still and the lake is calm, so it feels as if I'm inside a huge gray sphere and I hate gray!

The only life I can see in this world is a loon floating out in the middle of the lake so far away that it looks just like a black speck. I've been watching for a long time, almost hypnotized, thinking this lone loon fits perfectly with the melancholia that I am enjoying. I mean, it's the last day of the year. Let's have a little respect for the regrets, the lost dreams, the failures that we've experienced during the year – those letters that won't be written this year – those visits that won't be made this year. Goodness gracious, I think I'm going to start crying.

But wait a minute. There is not one loon, there are two. Winton just walked into the room and said, "What a wonderful gray afternoon this is!" Instead of crying I burst out laughing.

Somehow, knowing that the loon isn't pitifully alone makes all the difference in the world. It reminds me that we aren't either. Somehow, having my gray world invaded by a husband saying, "Isn't this gray world beautiful?" – did make it beautiful.

Our world is beautiful – "but" – forget the "but" – say it – "Our world is beautiful" – "but" – wait a minute – you see our precious Lord Jesus came into this world and cancelled the "but" for Christians. He has set things right! The year is ending and, alleluia, our walk with Jesus continues forever.

There are now three loons on the lake – naturally!

Your sister in Christ,

Lucy

Precious Group,

Winton and I were driving along a winding back-country road today, on the way to eating "good luck" black-eyed peas with friends. The sky was blue as blue could be, with not a cloud in the sky. The air was crisp and clean-smelling. The trees and ground looked wonderfully earthy. I mean it was a glorious day. We came over a hill and there on the right-hand side was a hand-painted sign saying, "Do Not Litter. This is God's Country!" I wanted to shout, "Amen, brother!" but restrained myself, for I would have had to find another ride to the party. Instead, I just inwardly smiled and thought, "Yes, Lord."

Earlier today we'd walked in the woods. I love rocks and Winton knew of some boulders that he wanted to show me. After thirty-five years of walking in the woods, I thought I knew every nook and cranny. Sure enough, set back in the trees, up a hill were three glorious boulders, heavily covered with moss and one had a carved-out spot you could sit in. Yea! How wonderful! Prettier than anything Rodin ever thought of sculpting!

"Do Not Litter. This is God's Country" – "Yes, Lord." I think that statement could be a colloquial version of **Exodus 3:5**: "Remove your sandals from your feet, for the place on which you are standing is holy ground."

My New Year's hope is that I will be more aware of the "holy ground" that surrounds me. It is very easy for me to worship my Creator God when I am surrounded by His natural beauty. I want it also, through His grace, to become easy for me to worship Him when I see His "human" beauty, for it is to these that the Lord God sent His Son.

You know what? I'm included in this group of "creations." Lucy, "Do Not Litter. This is God's Country." What I say, what I see, what I do – Lucy, "Do not litter. This is God's Country."

I think I've found my New Year's resolution – "Yes, Lord."

Your sister in Christ,

Lucy

Precious Group,

Anticipation. An-ti-ci-pa-tion…, as the commercial sings, is what I'm feeling right now! I'm so excited! We just hung up a bird feeder right outside the kitchen window. It was a wonderful surprise Christmas gift from some dear friends. When we arrived at the lake, there it was with a big red bow.

Of course, I wanted it to be instantly hanging on a tree ready to go – but no. It took two days till it reached its final resting place. We had to get the pliers, read the instructions, screw the two screws in just right, and discuss the location. Why, this was a very big project, even though it did come completely assembled and ready to go. It just was a slow "go."

Now I wait for a bird. Any old bird will do. In fact, I'll accept one small squirrel, if need be. I just want some wild life enjoying my gift. Anticipation.

It reminds me of every Christmas growing up. I was the youngest of the three children in my family and the rule was that no one could go downstairs Christmas morning until everyone was up. It drove me crazy! My older siblings, I think, were born slow, sophisticated, and not curious. It would take me at least four or five "bedroom attacks" before I could even get them out of their beds, much less walking and robed. Why, it truly was exhausting! Anticipation.

You know, anticipation is a wonderful state – it's bottled joy about to pop! Our oldest son is soon to be married. And I'm already anticipating grandchildren and what they'll call me… "Lulu," and what we'll play and dance and sing and….

And do you know what else? Our Lord and Saviour Jesus Christ is coming back – I mean talk about anticipation! I mean the "Lord of the Dance" is coming! That's why we can be people of joy!

Jesus says three times in the last chapter of Revelation, "I am coming quickly" – now that's something to anticipate!

Come on, birds – come on, Santa – come on, my Lord. I kneel with anticipation.

Your sister in Christ,

Lucy

Precious Group,

Have you ever had a magical person in your life? When you were with them the world was just a little bit brighter, a shine was on the ordinary, a giggle was constantly about to burst forth. Two such ladies come to my mind today. They never knew each other, but actually both were very similar. Both could have been Mrs. Santa Claus – short, a little plump, with creative gray hair (always a few wisps going the way they wanted), a little paint or glue on their fingers, eyes twinkled, a fast walk, for always busy – but never too busy to make me feel that they were sincerely glad to see me.

One was my friend and confidant during childhood – aunt Annie Paul Durr. She drove a "woody" station wagon, naturally. We made cookies for Christmas, blew out and decorated eggs for Easter. We played "doll house" together and made bookmarks and pin cushions and glittered anything that happened to need it. We made nut shells into gorgeous tree ornaments and she cried when I sang solos at church.

The other I met as a twenty-five-year-old grown-up when we were moving from Lakeland, Florida, to Montgomery. I went house hunting. Instead of a house, I came upon another magical lady – Lida Holly. I loved her house, but it only had three bedrooms and having a family of six, Winton said this wouldn't do. Lida also said this wouldn't do. In fact, she wanted me to forget this house, but come look at her paintings! The joy, the giggles, the sense of humor in each little jewel. There was always a story behind each one. It was better than Disney World. The "Magical Kingdom" reigned right there on Woodley Road in that precious lady's mind.

Both of these sparkles are sparkling in a different world now and I miss them. Yesterday I set up a miniature world which they both would have approved. Lida's daughter had given me a painting that Lida had painted of the lake. It is the background of the "magical world" and in front are little pine cone creatures – deer, pigs, raccoons, and rabbits that could have been made by Annie Paul. This world is, of course, behind closed doors – all magical worlds are. It is in the children's bathroom off the kitchen.

I bet one day a child (or a grown-up) will be in there and laugh and giggle and feel warmth and safety from that little scene – just as my ladies radiated – just as Christ radiated – just as we are to radiate.

"Let your light so shine before men that they may see your good works and glorify your Father which is in heaven." **Matthew 5:16.**

Your sister in Christ,

Lucy

Precious Group,

We have a new kitchen. I've never had a new kitchen before. Everything is shining and slick and clean. I mean, it's gorgeous! I mean nothing squeaks or is stopped up or scratched or stained. In fact, it really doesn't look like I belong in it and I'm going to try to keep it this way as long as I can. I've only started one kitchen fire in four months, so there is just one stove eye liner that is black. For this, I am truly thankful and proud!

Why, you could take a picture of this kitchen and put it in any fancy magazine, except, I think, they would insist on one change – "the red plastic solo cup, containing one red silk rose will have to go!" But I would protest, "You want a picture, then the tacky arrangement stays!"

"But Mrs. Blount, we thought you were a renowned English flower arranger! This does not live up to your tasteful standards!"

"Sorry – you'll have to find yourself another 'gorgeous gourmet galley.' This rose grows in my kitchen!"

A rose is a rose is a rose...

Mary Barwick

You've got to make your own fun.

Mary Barwick

Now that they're gone, I can give you the inside scoop on the rose. During the halftime at my youngest son's high school Homecoming football game, each senior's mother was presented one silk rose. This is a big deal! I knew that because I had already been cherishing an identical rose that my second son had handed me on the football field three years earlier. So I knew how to treat that flower, or at least I thought I did.

But Winton had a better plan. The morning after the game – in the kitchen, there stood my silk rose in a red plastic "solo" cup full of water. Winton had lovingly placed it there the night before. At breakfast he walked over to this cup, leaned over, smelled the rose and said, "Gosh, it's lasting well!"

And it continues to flourish. The metal stem is starting to rust, but the bloom is still just a bud ready to pop. What's that statement about "beauty is in the eye of the beholder"? That rose á la solo cup is beautiful! It's brought me more joy than dozens of real roses. That precious man took something of value and made it even more valuable by caring for it. I would probably have added the rose to the drawer of hidden treasures, never to have been noticed again – but not now – now it's flourishing.

I thank the dear Lord that He looks on us as Winton did that rose. We might see "tacky" but God sees terrific and it's because of His perspective that we can flourish. Because of His gift – our Lord – we can thrive. Grow in His grace!

Your sister in Christ,

Lucy

Precious Group,

On our beach at the lake stands a bonfire, ready to be lit. In fact, it's been ready for four months. The original plan was that on Labor Day morning at sunrise we were to cook breakfast over the coals. It was a wonderful idea! There were thirty-two relatives who arrived in their P.J.'s and robes at 6:00 a.m. to watch the sunrise, but alas, no beautiful sunrise! The wind was howling, waves crashing, menacing clouds, freezing cold, but everyone was a great sport. We drank coffee. The children played "Lets Find Win" (our twenty-five-year-old son, who didn't want to be disturbed, had hidden and slept in the boathouse). We cooked breakfast in the kitchen, giggled and laughed and everyone was home and back in bed by 7:00. The "First Annual Labor Day Breakfast á la Sunrise" didn't go exactly as planned "sans sunrise," but was fun! And thus, there sits the bonfire, waiting to be lit.

I've always loved campfires. Somehow, they instantly create fun and intimacy. Somores, hot dogs, doughboys, marshmallows – sounds horrible, but if you add songs and friends, it's divine. As a child, I fondly remember them at camp and the lake, and as an adult we had campfires by a stream next to our house in Delaware. It was glorious, so "Come and have breakfast" over a campfire made total sense to me. An invitation you couldn't refuse.

That same invitation was offered almost two thousand years ago, "Come and have breakfast" (**John 21:12a**) to the disciples. It is one of the most beautiful scenes in the Bible and it feeds my soul. Can you imagine the scene? These precious men had lost their Saviour, their best friend, the one that they had so closely followed almost to the end. Oh, and that "almost to the end" was what they were stuck with for the rest of their lives. They had been willing to leave family, riches, tradition, make fools of themselves almost to the end.

So now the hurt was double. They had His death plus their denial. Oh, if they could just have said, "Lord forgive …Lord forgive." They all felt guilt, but Peter even more because he had denied the (his) Lord three times, just like Jesus said. But Peter loved Him – loved Him more than life itself – but he denied – "Oh Lord, forgive."

They went fishing. I go shopping or eating. It's the same. Let's keep on keeping on, even with the hurt. Oh, but the hurt hurts! "Lord forgive!" There's a fire glowing on the beach. It's the Lord – it's OK – we're OK – "Lord forgive."

"Come and have breakfast."

To his glory, I'm going to light that campfire.

Your sister in Christ,

Lucy

Precious Group,

I get claustrophobia. I think it started when I was a teenager. Three of us sneaked into a drive-in movie by hiding in a car trunk. (Please don't tell my mother and I have repented.) The driver wouldn't let us out for a long time, as a joke. Fun and games! Thus, I am stuck today with hating closed-in places. I don't like driving in tunnels and King Tut's exhibit gave me the creeps.

There is one profound exception and I do want to tell you about it – the Christian Catacombs. Winton and I were lucky enough to go to Rome last spring. It is the city of churches. We must have visited at least ten. I cannot describe their beauty. Each one trying to express adoration of God more deeply than the other. The windows, the spirals, the altars, the statues, the ceilings, the organs – all the glory! Generation after generation trying to express their love for their immortal, invisible, omnipotent God. Glorious!

And then there were the Catacombs. Floor after floor after floor of stacked empty graves. There must have been thirty of us in our group. The Catacombs are owned by the Papal State, so each tour is conducted by a priest. Ours was from India. We didn't need much light to see, for his face shown as he recreated the world in which these first Christians lived – the persecutions, the secrecy, the total commitment to their Saviour. The tombs are carved out of lava rock, stacked probably five high to the ceiling. We'd weave back and forth along narrow corridors on floor after floor, level after level.

Most of the tombs were empty because of the vandalism over the centuries and I'm glad, for it made their statement so much more poignant. Along a narrow way, we came into a larger space – a room. Again, empty tombs on all sides and in this holy space, we were told Christians met to worship. Somehow, this "church" outshone, for me, all the others. No windows, no spirals, no altars, but a room surrounded by empty tombs. It felt to me like Christ's tomb must have felt to the women.

"Don't be alarmed," he said. "You are looking for Jesus the Nazarene, who was crucified. He has risen! He is not here." **Mark 16:6a.**

What a monument! I've been to Indian burial grounds and Chinese emperors' tombs and felt nothing but claustrophobia. In the Catacombs it was different, for I knew that I was on hallowed ground. I let the group go on a little ahead. I stopped and prayed. Prayed for these saints who left no jewels or pottery or buried treasure behind, only empty tombs – as their Saviour had.

Hallelujah! "He has risen! He is not here!"

> Your sister in Christ,
> Lucy

Precious Group,

I've been walking with a dear friend for eight years. Rain, hail, sleet or snow… we walk. Monday through Friday, from 6:00 to 7:00 – we walk. We've solved many a global problem and a few family ones. We've remodeled husbands, houses, children, friends, enemies. In fact, we've gotten everything pretty much in shape, at least we thought so, for one hour a day. We usually walk and talk fast, fast, fast – and then we have "quiet time." The walk slows, the world slows. We refocus on our Lord and then the day begins. Bliss!

We've had many surprises during these times. A living Christmas tree covered with purple wisteria, an albino pigeon during Holy Week, which we swore was a white dove, a huge holly bush full of birds that sing, sing, sing – instantly stop when we arrive – then instantly continue to sing, sing, sing when we leave (we wonder who's the 'look-out' saying, "They're here"). We've come across a college campus laced in toilet paper and it was beautiful! Well, as you can tell we have truly seen some awesome sights!

Today was no exception. Fog – thick, deep, heavy fog. Wonderful fog. So many times in my life I've had to drive alone in fog, usually to Birmingham or the lake, hoping to find another car ahead so I could follow its lights. The most poignant time that I remember was driving to see my daddy in the hospital. The fog made my already fearful spirit more afraid until I turned up the praise music and turned my eyes to the Lord. The fog lifted and the sun came out. I like fog, for it narrows my world down and refocuses me.

Anyway, Madeliene and I were walking in this close world, feeling like a down comforter had gently been laid over us, when we came upon a stuffed animal lying in the road, a one-eyed monkey with arms stretched out. Madeliene said it was saying, "Help me!" So we picked it up out of the road and placed it on the grass. Another monkey saved by the morning troops.

We then passed by the movie theatre which was playing "A Long White Season." Now where are we going – where am I going? **Luke 24:13-53:** Emmaus. My mind focuses on those two Christians walking together. The fog might not have been hanging outside, but I bet inside their souls were feeling fogged in. They'd lost their friend, their companion, their Messiah. Here they were grieving together, reliving their shared tragedy, comforting each other, and here comes a man barging into their intimate space who not only isn't invited, but doesn't know anything about it! (Winton would ask, "Didn't you read the newspaper?") Jesus walks with them, listens to their version of the story, then tells His, explains the scripture, then breaks the bread. The fog lifts.

The fog is lifting. Light brings the world back into focus. Jesus brings our world back into focus. The fears, the anxieties lose their grip on our lives. We are those "one-eyed monkeys" with arms reaching out for help. And we have it!

Luke 24:29-31a: "And they urged Him, saying stay with us for it is getting toward evening and the day is now nearly over. And He went in to stay with them. And it came about that when He had reclined at the table with them, He took the bread and blessed it and breaking it, He began giving it to them. And their eyes were opened and they recognized Him."

The fog lifts in His light! Good morning, Lord!

Your sister in Christ,

Lucy

Precious Group,

"Come unto me, all ye that labour and are heavy laden, and I will give you rest." **Matthew 11:28.**

Boy, that's good news! Lord, I'm tired — bone tired — both mentally and spiritually tired. At a conference for the past ten hours, I've been informed of the problems in our city. I mean weighed down, burdened and wrung out! A glimmer of hope would almost flicker then — whomp! put out by a "but." Crime, drugs, economics, education, government, racism, sexism — whomp! I feel like I have been bombed by reality. My beautiful bubble has popped, or has it? And if it has, what's left — a puddle? No! A cross — two crosses.

The facilitator ended the sessions by drawing two pluses (++) on the blackboard and concluded that in all situations, the only way for progress is a "win-win" situation. He saw two pluses — I saw two crosses — one Christ's — the other mine. He saw every unjust, evil situation in our society as having to do with power play, and he felt that only as we eliminate the power over one another can positive change be made. He saw two pluses, I saw two crosses — Jesus' and mine. He hoped some day our group could embrace each other and accept each other's differences. I saw Jesus washing feet (**John 13:5**) — and talk about reverse power play — Jesus washing feet.

I've only had a "foot washing" with five-year-olds and I love five-year-olds. They're usually game for anything. "A foot washing, yea!" It was during Bible School. I got my group seated in a circle, some giggling, some timid. While taking off their shoes, I received wonderful comments like "ucky!" On my knees I went around washing their precious little feet with soap and water and telling them that Jesus did this to show His disciples that He loved them. Some squirmed at first, complaining of tickles, then slowly they became quiet and attentive. "Oh, Jesus did this!"

I wish I'd had a bucket of water today at the meeting. I could feel the hurt and the pain and the anger and the frustration. Two pluses — two crosses — Jesus' and mine.

"People, roll up your pants, sit back, relax, take your shoes and socks off, I've got something better than a hug."

Two pluses — no — two crosses — Jesus' and mine.

"Take up your cross and follow me." **Mark 8:34.**

Yes, Lord. Do you mind if I bring a bucket of water along?

Your sister in Christ,

Lucy

Precious Group,

I got a "demo" this week.

The last car I'd had for five years was a red Blazer. It had a lot of personality. It was dented from a hail storm. The speedometer could do a dance all the way around the gauge. The horn worked when it felt like it. The radio had a little man in it who would change the station every time I got out of the car. The back window had a built-in guillotine window. There were leftover stickers on the visor so I knew who I was and where I'd been. A round rock, given to me by my middle son, along with sticky money, resided in the seat divider. The smell (created by hundreds of buckets of water spilling over from carting flowers) outdid any skunk — so only real friends would ride with me. I mean it took me a long time to get this car "broken-in" just right!

Now I have a "demo" — shiny, clean, raring to go — but with one big drawback — it's not mine. There can be no stickers — no food or drink creatively partaken — no sticky money — no buckets of water and after four thousand miles, I have to give it back. You see, I have to take real good care of it, for it's not mine.

My mind jumps to Lazarus — I wonder about Lazarus. I wonder what it was like coming from that tomb — in death — in total darkness — having the burial clothes unwound — then seeing Jesus, whose light infused him back to life. He probably blinked his eyes, trying to get used to the light and felt the warmth of his blood once more flowing and then he saw Jesus — his friend — his Lord — with a tear in His eye — smiling.

Do you think Lazarus saw his body and life differently after having died? Do you think he took better care of it — was more aware of the preciousness of life — of friends — of loved ones? Do you think that seeing Jesus with a tear was stamped indelibly on his brain, so that everything he did and said was from then on filtered through this experience?

The Bible says I must be born again — that I am to die unto self — that I am a new creature in Christ — that I am not my own, but Christ's.

All of these verses make me think about my red demo and how I am to care for it, for it's not mine. All of these verses make me think of "me" and how I am to care for "me," for I am not mine.

Lazarus — Lucy — A Demo. I think we have more in common than meets the eye.

I've got a "demo" which is not mine. What are you going around in?

> Your sister in Christ,
>
> Lucy

Precious Group,

I just talked to my mother on the phone. She told me that yesterday she went to a luncheon and that a seventy-nine-year-old lady died in her arms.

"Mama, what did you do?"

"I acted like a grown-up."

In awe, I said, "Ohhh!"

Grown-up — gosh that's a hard concept for the youngest in the family to comprehend. I've always understood Peter Pan's retreating back to Never-Never Land. "Wendy, forget it! I'll take the lost boys and Tinkerbell and flying any day over your grown-up world!" — makes total sense to me.

Grown-up, what does that mean? I know at forty-one, I might need to consider this term — not necessarily adopt it, you understand, for I am the youngest and the cutest and I like that position.

But what about understanding it? "I'll try — Lord — I'll try — just for a little while." I guess if I had to pick a "grown-up" to study, it would have to be John the Baptist. He amazes me. This man would not be someone you would want as a dinner partner. Besides having peculiar eating habits, I bet he didn't participate in trivial chit-chat. I bet sparks came out of him — left and right — cutting through phoniness. It would be worse than when I had Barishnikov as my dinner partner and I was as cute as a Southern Belle could be, short of grabbing his leg, and he just yawned and kept looking around. My ESP told me he was thinking "Jessica (Lang), where are you? Let me out of here!"

I think John the Baptist would have gotten up and left — for this was a man with a mission — driven. He had a purpose that so forged his life that he knew his goal and went for it — 100%. I mean, "Go for the Gusto" is a weak statement when you think of this man!

He's like a runner who runs as fast as he can, with all his might, then hands the baton to the next runner. "He must increase, but I must decrease." **John 3:30.** That's an amazing statement to me. It is totally foreign to every message we receive in this "me" oriented world — but it does make sense in the light of Jesus.

I'm starting to experience this "decreasing" myself with my daughter — she's a beautiful young woman of twenty-two. I used to show her how to put on make-up, she now shows me. I used to show her how to cook, she now shows me. And I'm sure when she has children, she'll tell me how to take care of them. It's fun. It's the way it should be. "He must increase, but I must decrease."

I think that's what being a "grown-up" must be – letting go – letting God. When John the Baptist was in prison, all he wanted from Jesus was assurance– not freedom – but assurance. **Matthew 11:2-6:** "Are you the Christ?" And Jesus responded by having His disciples tell John what Jesus was doing – everything which the Old Testament foretold.

Mama was a "grown-up" yesterday. I think that lady got a decreased Mama, which allowed an increased Jesus to shine through. The lady went from one person's arms into another pair, similar, but larger.

Lord, may I grow-up? May I decrease and You increase?

Your sister in Christ,

Lucy

Precious Group,

What a gloriously beautiful day! I just drove up to the lake and was fortunate to time it just right so that I could listen to one of my favorite radio personalities, "Mrs. G." Every Saturday morning at 9:30, Mrs. G. tells children's bible stories in the most enchanting manner. She sounds like a wonderful grandmother with a British accent. I can imagine sitting curled up in her lap, with her arms around me, as she brings to life Jesus and His world.

She reminds me of my ninety-four-year-old grandmother for whom I am named. She lived with us while I was growing up, and one of my favorite activities was to listen to her tell stories as she braided her waist-length hair. It was a warm time – a close time – a safe time. The story would invariably end with a "happy ever after" and the braid would become a crown or a halo, depending on the tale.

Spontaneous storytelling from one you love is grand! It's not so much the story, as the intimate bond that exists. It's like receiving a rare gift from one you love.

I think that was the atmosphere which prevailed when Jesus said, "Suffer the little children to come unto me." **Matthew 19:14**. As a child, this was the first mental picture I had of Jesus. Me – sitting in His lap – receiving love. Sometimes in my mind, I'd squirm and get down and twirl for Him and then crawl back up into His arms. He'd be smiling – understanding that I had a very short attention span and would have to fidget. But that was OK – I was only a child – I am only a child.

Then as a "grown-up" listening to Jesus, I pictured myself as Mary, sitting at His feet – listening – adoring – absorbing every story He had to tell, for I knew this could not last (**Luke 10:39**). I had to help Martha, I had to become Martha very shortly. My daily schedule only permitted Mary a short visit, for Martha had a list of things to be done. He would tell His story – I'd listen, I'd adore. He'd smile – I'd smile and I'd hear Martha coming. But that was OK. I was only a grown-up.

Then as a sinner – I don't like to talk about that state. I don't like to come to Jesus in that state – but I do.

Not able to look Him in the face... Not able to climb into His lap... Not able to sit at His feet – for I am ashamed. I can only touch His hem (**Mark 5:28**). I know if I look up, I'll see Him smiling.

"But Lord – I was a child, I was a grown-up, I was a sinner."

"But Lord – I <u>am</u> a child, I <u>am</u> a grown-up, I <u>am</u> a sinner."

"That's OK? You want me to climb up into your lap anyway?"

"Will you give me a hand?"

"Oh, a cross."

"Yes, Lord. I'm climbing."

Your sister in Christ,

Lucy

Precious Group,

I have the flu – headache, fever, cough – that achey feeling. I'd be perfect for one of those pitifully unattractive ads on TV, but the remedies which I would promote can't be bought at the pharmacist. Here are Lucy's Flu Fighters:

First, I called up and cancelled all of my appointments for the day. Amazingly, the world will continue without me.

Second, I got a good book. Oh, the luxury of a good book! This one was truly delicious. I would read a few pages – drift off to sleep – then read – then drift. I even slowed this snail-pace reading down as I approached the end, for it was so wonderful.

Third, I've eaten at least a crate of oranges, so that our bedroom is starting to smell kind of tropical.

Fourth, I've stared out the window – no really picturesque sight in this 4'x6' world: blue sky, winter tree branches, and a white column which helps hold up our house.

I feel like everything is in slow motion. (I've only had aspirin.) My breathing is slow, my mind is slow, my world is slow, and the only motion I occasionally see is a bird flying to my visible branches. Everything else is still. I am aware of the changing light and the changing shadows during the day. I absorb the warmth coming through the window. I feel like I'm a sponge, absorbing energy – absorbing God.

It's been a long time since I've had a daily still. I totally comprehend the command, "Be still and know that I am God." When we're almost shut down, the vitality of God is so much more real.

Once, after an operation, I spent a whole week of recuperation on a floor pallet. Daily, I looked out the window and had the joy of watching a tulip tree bring forth its blossoms. It was fantastic. I love to watch nature films which use time-lapse photography. Miracles take place right before your eyes. Because of an operation and a "slow me down, Lord" attitude, I now better understand that tulip tree. We share a secret — I have seen its blessings come forth. Right now its buds are tight once more — but I know there are blossoms within and it brings me joy, even in this secret state, as it never has before.

The sun has finally come to my window world. I knew it was hovering close, because of the light, but now it has entered, shining and brilliant. I can't look out now, for it's too bright, but I can shut my eyes and then take in the sights with my interior eyes. This world is red and warm with little squiggles drifting by. I like this window sunbathing — it feels healing and God is present.

I don't want to be building this flu up too much. Forget the flu — it's a drag, but the slowing down of my world that it affords is a blessing. I do recommend pulling up a chair to a window and sitting for a day, or a half day or even an hour. I'm sure you have a window world that is anxious to share its secrets with you, but most importantly, you have an Almighty God who commands, "Be still, and know that I am God."

Freeze, and relish the Almighty.

Your sister in Christ,

Lucy

Precious Group,

It's my mama's seventieth birthday today. Out of celebration, I would like each one of you to put this love letter down and with great gusto, sing "Happy Birthday" to Mama. After completion, I request that you stoop down into a crouched position and then do a jack-in-the-box jump, as high as you can. At the zenith of your jump, please muster up all of your cheerleading skills and enthusiastically yell — "Whee!" — that's right, "Whee!"

This exercise is not only good for your cardiovascular system, but is also an appropriate tribute to Mama, for this has been her battle cry for as long as I can remember. Whenever we came upon beauty or surprise or joy, Mama couldn't help but come forth with a "Whee!" In fact, it has become such a family tradition with my own group, that whenever we gather, we end meal blessings with "Whee!" instead of "Amen." Try it. It's also a great substitute for "Allelujah" or "Thank you, Lord" or "Praise Jesus!" and it doesn't get half the stares. That's what I'd

like to do today – a big "Praise Jesus" – a big "Thank You, Lord" – a big "Whee!" for my Mama.

Right now I'm riding and writing in a white convertible, with the top down. It is so much fun! I haven't ridden in one since I was sixteen years old. We just came to a quick halt because five deer jumped across the road – I mean a four-point "Whee!" Grand! They must know it's Mama's birthday, too!

Back to celebration! I have a mental "Daddy picture" that I carry. I also hold one of my mama. It was taken on Christmas Eve about 1958. Our family always had the Christmas Eve Party and all friends and relatives were invited. The star of the night, was, of course, baby Jesus and we would sing His Christmas carols.

The other star I remember was Mama. Each Christmas Eve Daddy would give her a gorgeous new dress for her to wear to the party. It would be made of chiffon or silk or satin and often jeweled. This particular 1958 dress was strapless, white silk, to the floor and had panels of cut-velvet roses down the back. In the picture we're standing facing each other and it is obvious from my adoring gaze that I knew she was the most beautiful mother in the world.

And today, to me, she continues to be the most beautiful mother in the world! You know the number seven is very significant in our Bible tradition. It is the number that stands for completion. Of course, Mama isn't complete – yet. She won't be in this world – not until her eternal birthday – but her beauty is getting deeper and deeper. The strapless dress was grand and becoming – but today her beauty is so much more glorious.

I love the last chapter in **Proverbs 31**. So many of the verses seem to be speaking specifically about Mama. "A capable, intelligent and virtuous woman." – "She is far more precious than jewels and her value is far above rubies or pearls." – "She opens her hand to the poor, yes, she reaches out her filled hands to the needy." – "Strength and dignity are her clothing and her position is strong and secure; she rejoices over the future." – "She opens her mouth in skillful and godly wisdom, and on her tongue is the law of kindness." – "She looks well to how things go in her household, and the bread of idleness she will not eat." – "Her children rise up and call her blessed and her husband boasts of and praises her." – "Many daughters have done virtuously, nobly and well, but you excel them all."

May we pause – for all the Mama's – for all the women of virtue – for all the shining stars. May we get into a crouched position – do a "jack-in-the-box" jump as high as we can, and with all the cheerleading skills we can muster – yell, "Whee!" (Amen, Allelujah, Thank you, Lord, Praise Jesus!)

Especially today for Beverley White Dunn – alias Mama. Happy Birthday!

Your daughter and sister in Christ,
Lucy

Precious Group,

I'm on the way to the Big Apple. New York City, here I come! This place has always been thrilling for me. I remember my first trip with my family at nine years old. I knew it was a big deal and something grand was getting ready to happen for I had "Traveling Clothes." I'd never had "Traveling Clothes" before. One was a navy tailored dress and one was a green tailored dress. I was a little plump, so tailored was important and dark, I learned, was important, in case there were mishaps – like spills or crumbs. I think the "Dark Traveling Clothes" must have originated with the Pilgrims or at least with my grandmother, who always safely arrived for a visit in a "Dark Traveling Suit." You know the road from Uniontown to Birmingham (two hours) was treacherous and could only be safely driven in "Dark Clothes." Proudly, I continue the family tradition. I'm in a "Dark Traveling Suit," so I know a spot-free, safe arrival is guaranteed.

I've always had the eyes of "Eloise" of the Plaza Hotel fame when it comes to N.Y.C. I share her enthusiasm over the big and the little of New York. I still walk down the streets with my mouth open, staring up – in awe – at its bigness – the buildings, lights, theaters, restaurants, people. I also stare in awe of its littleness – the neighborhood groceries, the little families in the park, the carriage drivers, the hot dog venders, the bag ladies. How can all these people live in this hugeness – in their littleness? It's amazing to me.

Well – I'm off. I'm getting ready to land – my littleness in this huge bigness. Thank goodness, I'm meeting Mama. We can handle anything together – including N.Y.C. I mean – we three – Lord be with us.

I'm now safely situated in our room waiting for Mama to arrive. While waiting for my bags at the airport, I counted crosses for fun. There were a lot of them. Three nuns, I know, were genuine and the others might have mainly been Madonna fans, but praise the Lord – His cross is being worn. I spoke to the cleaning lady in the bathroom – she almost fainted, but finally warmed and spoke to me. My taxi driver had the only taxi whose meter didn't work. "Ah hah!

Another dumb Southerner!" My mother had already informed me of the correct fare. He reluctantly agreed to it – then I tipped him $5.00, just for the joy. He smiled – I smiled – and swinging my cross said, "Have a nice day." He possibly thought, "I not only got a dumb one – but a religious nut, too!" I do know his smile was genuine.

It's not my intent to just write "warm fuzzies" to you or a "Travels with Lucy" journal. It is my intent to point to our Almighty God as He reveals Himself to me in this world. Omnipotent – Omniscient – Omnipresent – Creator – Comforter – Counselor – our Strength – our Redeemer – our Lord. There's no way words can capture the uncapturable. I can adore – we can adore. "We are His people and the sheep of His pasture." I thank God for that. I thank God for our Shepherd. Now I'm going to see if this room has a Gideon – rejoice! We are His!

I'm now stuck in the Atlanta airport on the way home. They're working on our airplane. A man sitting nearby said, "The rubber band must have broken," – back to reality. The trip was glorious. To have quality visiting time alone with Mama was wonderful – to just share our love and our memories was grand. We revisited Radio City Music Hall to see the Moscow Circus. Because of a three-year-old child sitting next to me, I was allowed to enter back into the childhood wonder of it all. When he clapped – I clapped. When he laughed – I laughed. His grandfather answered brilliantly all of his "why" questions – including, "The reason for starting the performance at 3:30 was that the elephants had to take a nap and they were just now having their juice and cookies and would then be ready to start." Made sense to me!

The only other insight I'd like to share is that we visited with two New Yorkers – one a cousin, another a friend. One thing that they shared in their metropolitan living was having no views from their apartments. You could only see buildings out of all other windows, except for one. My cousin was very proud that you could put your head out of the living room window and lean just right and see Central Park. I said, "how nice" – but thought, "how enclosing." If my whole home-world was visually man-made, I think I would go crazy!

Or would I? I woke up this morning at 6:30. My bed was right next to the window overlooking the park. I didn't want to awaken Mama, so I just lay there until she woke at 8:00. The window shade was drawn. The room was in total darkness. As the morning broke, the light haloed around the shade. I wanted so badly to draw up the shade or peek under it – but, no – I just looked at that drawn shade, which blocked out the light. I thought of those buildings and apartments that blocked out the views and the "Light." Then I thought on the scripture **Matthew 27:50-51:** "And Jesus cried again with a loud voice and gave up His Spirit. And at once the curtain of the sanctuary of the temple was torn in two from top to bottom: the earth shook and the rocks split."

For all eternity, the curtain has been torn – the "Light" has come into the world – the victory is won. As Christians, there is no building – no window shade – no experience – that can block us from the "Light" – from His view. The curtain has been eternally torn – the Holy One Shines!

My flight was canceled. We taxied onto the runway and the pilot said he didn't have enough "right engine" to take off. We taxied back to the airport. I ran to another flight – was put on stand-by – didn't make it. Now after four hours waiting, I'm in the air. I wish I could make an announcement on the speaker: "Ladies and Gentlemen, we have the Right Engine – Ladies and Gentlemen, we have the Right Light – Ladies and Gentlemen, we have a 'Room with a View' – for all eternity. Thank you and have a nice flight – home."

Your sister in Christ,

Lucy

Precious Group,

The flight from Montgomery to Atlanta was the roughest flight that I've ever been on. When we landed, the stewardess went to check on each passenger, asked if we were all right and gathered up the little white bags on her mission of mercy. I made the flight with a cross in one hand and "the bag" in the other.

I knew that I was supposed to be on that flight. It had a 5:45 a.m. departure time. My alarm clock didn't go off, but the Lord woke me up just in time to make it. I didn't know why, but as we were wildly gyrating – I knew God wanted me right there. All I could say is "O.K. Lord, I'm here. I don't want to be here. Please calm my stomach, my mind and this sky!" What made me laugh was that four days previously, I swore that I would never get on this particular airline again and here I was, strapped in once more.

My trust level was total, for I had no other choice. That total surrender to the situation – to God – was humbling. I had no control. It was God and the pilot. That was a good exercise for me – a total letting go. I bet my daily "flights" would go a lot smoother if I had that same mind-set – that same letting go – that same "Pilot." (We did make it. I found out later that the reason it was so rough was that there were tornados all around. Great!)

On the next leg of the flight it was smooth sailing. As I was having my daily quiet time and Bible reading, my seatmate, who was a very distinguished sixty-five-year-old Swiss banker, mentioned that he was fluent in seven languages, one of which was Aramaic. "Excuse me? There were three hundred people on this airplane and the one I have the privilege of sitting next to writes and speaks Aramaic? O.K., everyone who speaks Aramaic, raise your hand?" (my interior conversation) – exterior, I laughed and almost attacked him. I felt there were not going to be a lot of opportunities to hear Jesus' native language, so I had him to say and write "Lo, I am with you always." **Matthew 28:20.** I chose that scripture because that's what I want to always know. When the Alzheimers hits or right before I cross over the bar, the last earthly thought I want is "Lo, I am with you always."

This verse has always been a great comfort to my mother. She had a difficult delivery of my brother: a thirty-six-hour labor and a breech birth. As they wheeled her into the delivery room, over the door was written, "Lo, I am with you always." Nineteen years later that son was killed in a motorcycle accident and a chapel was given in his memory. On the altar kneeler, in needlepoint, reads, "Lo, I am with you always."

The man said and wrote that verse. He then said "Here, let me write 'The Lord is risen from the dead.'" "Yes, that would be nice," I replied. He asked my name and wrote "ee ell" = Lucy. We then were quiet. He slept – I floated. I also kept asking the Lord, what should I write to you? My "white bag" experience hadn't brought any scripture to mind. The only scene which kept surfacing all week was Jesus – drawing in the dirt while the crowd, with clinched rocks, taunted the adulteress. But I wasn't sure. **John 8:3-11.**

My seatmate awoke and out of the blue asked, "Where is that scripture about Mary Magdalene being stoned located in the Bible?" I almost dropped The Book! O.K. Lord – we'll look. **John 8:6.** This scene came to my mind earlier this week while participating in my first "march." I didn't feel the march was something that I wanted to share with you, for I felt that it was too political – too controversial – might alienate you instead of encouraging you. As you can tell by my letters, I am a peacemaker, by gift and nature.

There are some observations I can share with you though – and here goes. Thirty-five thousand people walking together in purpose. There was a calm – a joy – a feeling that this was good and right. Smiles – singing – down-right fun – children everywhere – walking with a best friend and a godson – meeting fellow Christians – Episcopal clergy – it was grand! The only other march I had been close to was in 1970 at the University of Alabama. Then I observed from a rooftop an angry mob protesting Vietnam. The feeling was entirely different. Back to this week's march: we arrived at the Capitol. Being short and in the back of the crowd, I couldn't see the speakers. While listening, I looked down and there were children playing in the dirt. On hands and knees, building gorgeous dirt mounds and finger roads. Jesus drawing with His finger on the ground (**John 8:6**) surrounded by an angry crowd, popped into my mind.

This march versus the Vietnam march...

The children drawing in the dirt versus Jesus drawing in the dirt...

The crowds were different, the circumstances were different...

For me, the difference was Christ. Two thousand years ago an angry crowd wanted to stone a woman. Christ wrote in the dirt. They hurled insults – He looked up and offered love and forgiveness. The anger dissolved and the crowd dispersed.

1970 – an angry crowd gathered, marched and I felt fear.

1990 – a crowd gathered, marched and the children drew in the dirt.

I wonder – who taught them that this was what one does when a crowd gathers? I wonder – who brought this feeling of joy and calm and play? I wonder –

Jeremiah 31:3: "The Lord appeared to him from afar saying, I have loved you with an everlasting love; therefore I have drawn you with loving-kindness."

Jesus stooped down and wrote on the ground – the children continue the drawing – I wonder.

Your sister in Christ,

Lucy

Precious Group,

I am at an "Oasis" in the desert. It's morning. I've turned my chair to the window – drinking my coffee – reading my scripture – talking to the Lord – listening. I guess you can tell in my world there's a lot of "get up and go" in my life. I thank the Dear Lord for that. I thank the Dear Lord for the privilege of getting to see so many wonderful sights in His world – of getting beds turned down by the "mint fairy" who leaves her treasure of two candies (which I flush down the toilet) – of getting little baskets from the hotel bunny with goodies of soap, shampoo, needle and thread.

It took some getting used to, of dropping in and out and around and about, every other week – for you see, I'm a "nester." I like digging in – my flannel nightgown with socks – my dog sleeping at the foot of my bed – my routine morning walk with my friend, Mad – my routine church – my routine choir – my routine everything. I am a creature of habit and I thrive in the routineness of it all. I've learned to stop trying to sell "poor pitiful Lucy – I've got to go on another trip" – for it doesn't work. Most people want to go. They want to get out of their nests for a breather and I understand that – it's just that I get out of breath sometimes.

Oasis in the night.

Mary Barwick

So what do I do? I turn my chair to the window. Wherever we go, one of the first things I do is to stake a claim on a spot for my nesting ground – my centering spot – where I can be quiet with the Lord and absorb His routineness.

It's 8:30 a.m. in LaQuinta, California. My precious Winton had a 7:15 meeting and he just returned. My window nest is built right at the front door. I'm sitting in my hotel-provided white robe with my brown plastic raincoat used as a lap robe. The room is small, so he had to maneuver himself around me to enter. I love that precious man. He's getting used to me after twenty years. He thinks my nesting is normal – that everyone lounges in brown plastic and terry each morning. I thank the Lord for him!

Now back to the oasis in the desert. You have never seen such beauty. I'm looking at green grass, bougainvillea, and palm trees – against a backdrop of blue sky and desert mountains. It's the two sharply different worlds juxtaposed to each other that makes the beauty so intense – so unreal – so screaming out at each other – "Look at me." – "No, you look at me!"

My reading for this morning was about Esau and Jacob. **Genesis 25:29-34.** Esau sold Jacob his birthright. He was hungry, starving – wanted immediate relief – immediate gratification. "I want what I want now." So he sold his birthright. He jumped from his desert of hunger to his lentil soup oasis – but it was just a mirage. He settled for second best or less. How often do we do this? How often, when we are in our "desert" state of mind, do we settle for a "mirage" for relief?

There is only one true "Oasis" – no palm trees – but a cross for shelter – and that's sufficient. **II Corinthians 12:9:** "My grace is sufficient for you, for power is perfected in weakness." Now that's an Oasis!

Your sister in Christ,

Lucy

Precious Group,

I want to tell you about the desert. I want you to be able to feel the heat – the dryness – the desolation. Yesterday we walked for two hours in this world – into the mountains – down into a canyon. At one point, we could only get through the pass by turning sideways. Looking up, you could only see a sliver of light. Then we had to get on our stomachs and crawl like animals to get through the opening. We were right on the San Andreas Fault. The intensity of the squeeze mentally was just as oppressive as this physical squeeze.

I wanted this experience. The desert had been calling to me just as the ancient Sirens of Greek mythology. From the moment we flew over this arid world, I knew I wanted to get this world under my skin so that I might better understand it at a deeper level.

I'd experienced the desert once before when we visited Saudi Arabia. August in Saudi is truly a desert experience. But I didn't get to relish it, to let it infiltrate me, for I was more concerned about our daughter having a heat stroke. None of my family would fall for, "Hey, let's spend the day in the desert." Instead it was more like, "Mom, if we don't get air conditioning real soon, you're going to have a mutiny on your hands!"

But yesterday was different. I went to the desert and relished it. Abraham – Isaac – Jacob – Joseph – Moses – the Israelites – these people marched in my brain. God over and over used this world to fine tune His people – to forge them into iron. They became purposed – driven – obsessed – loyal – humble – reverent people – His people. Paul and the desert fathers of early Christianity all went to the desert for that very same reason – refinement – re-centering. Today in this twentieth century world, we go to a spa to get rejuvenated. I question whether "refinement" in the desert might be time better spent.

Back to the belly crawl. I've always felt squeezed by **Matthew 19:24** – "It is easier for a camel to go through the eye of a needle, than for a rich man to enter the kingdom of God." I've always dwelled on the first part of the scripture and felt fat and not listened to Christ say (**Matthew 19:26b**), "With men this is impossible, but with God all things are possible." Crawling on my belly – through this needle eye in the desert, a light bulb came on in my mind. "Hey, there's room enough – that's all you need – room enough!" Also, we're told our walk is to be "straight and narrow." I used to see that as limiting – but it's not – it's good news! It's more direct – no room for wasted energy!

The canyon was straight and narrow and O.K. At first, I saw very little life in this world, but an excellent guide showed us that the desert was a veritable supermarket and could meet all of our needs if we knew where to shop. There were ten of us following the guide. We couldn't help but play "follow the leader" – there was no other choice – no room for an alternative route. Oh, if we could have that reality in Christ. No other route but His – in every situation of our lives – His route – His path.

I believe that when Jesus came out of the desert, He brought with Him that "desert reality" for the rest of His life. His purpose was etched indelibly in His mind. His road was straight and narrow – One Way – His Father's.

I believe that's what deserts produce – a setting of boundaries and limits – a refinement of purpose. We all don't have a Coachela Desert or an Arabian Desert in our backyards to foster this experience. Our deserts are more interior, life-produced – by interior or exterior situations and circumstances. I believe the Holy Spirit – the Bible – the Church – can show us the straight and narrow way. Our Guide is our Christ.

In the hotel sitting room where I'm writing, there is a lush garden mural over the fireplace with the inscription "Jardin de mes Ensueños" which means "Garden of my Dreams." I believe our deserts lead to such a place, as long as we follow our Guide – our Christ.

He says daily, "I am the way, and the truth, and the life; no one comes to the Father, but through Me." **John 14:6**.

Yesterday, I went to the desert and had an excellent guide who knew the way. But the fantastic good news is today and all my tomorrows and yours, we have The Guide – our Lord Jesus – who is the Way! Lord may we follow!

Your sister in Christ,

Lucy

Precious Group,

My prayer this morning has been "Lord, on you may I lean and thus not jam!" Have you ever seen a log jam on a river? It's a big pile up – a big mess! When there's a jam-up and all of that energy goes astray, you have the ultimate beaver dam – I mean a mess!

Today, I was headed for a jam-up. The busyness of my world was crashing in on me. I felt like it must be Christmas in February. The lists were building in my mind. The tune which kept playing in my brain was "The Twelve Days of Christmas" – two trips to Birmingham, three classes to attend, four suitcases to pack, five letters to write – over and over and over.

A log jam versus a smooth flowing of logs, which is awesome. When done right, a little tugboat pulls or pushes, depending on the maneuver, thousands of logs with apparent ease. They are encircled by a cable and that little tugboat gets those logs to their correct destination. All of that energy correctly channeled almost adds beauty to the river – it blends in with the flow. But I was headed for a log jam!

When I was in Canada watching the logs float on the Campbell River, the most amazing maneuver to me was the one the pilot performed over the rapids. It was a powerful river. It would be smooth-flowing and you'd come around a bend and there would be white caps and churning whirlpools. Situated near the bank of the bend, completely stopped, waiting out the dramatic tides, winds, and rough water, would be a little tugboat, with his logs just sitting there waiting. His load was totally under control – totally still. Eagles soared, fishing boats bounced – motion everywhere – but the tugboat and his load stood still.

It had the potential of producing the most energy, the most force in that bend. If unleashed, those logs could have acted like the ultimate bowling balls, knocking over every boat in sight – but the pilot kept the logs contained, orderly, under control – until the river was right for his load. But I am headed for a log jam!

One of my least-favorite Jesus scenes has always been when the young man was called by Jesus to follow – and the young man responded – "Lord, permit me first to go and bury my Father." Our Lord responded with "Follow Me; and allow the dead to bury their own dead." **Matthew 8:21-22**. I've always thought, "How cold!" How could my Lord Jesus respond so heartlessly. Surely Matthew made a mistake! My loving Lord wouldn't act like that! Probably at this point in His life, His own father had died. After having personally experienced such a heartache, such a loss myself, I know you have empathy for others. You meet them in their pain – feel it – share it – try to defuse it. If I know this, in my brokenness, I knew Jesus knew.

So what's going on here? My Jesus, the ultimate defuser, wouldn't respond this way. Surely something else was going on – surely! Looking closer, I believe His eyes had tears in them and His arms were around the young man. There was total empathy to such a level that we will never be able to emulate. He not only felt it but absorbed the pain. The funeral preparations, the lists, the busyness, the log jam which the man was forming in his mind, Christ took it all to the cross. He became the Pilot and said in love, with deep compassion – quietly – reassuringly – "Follow Me; and allow the dead to bury their dead."

The log jam dissolved – my log jam is dissolving.

The order flowed – my order flows.

The pilot steered – my Pilot steers.

How does that song, "Up a Lazy River," go?

Flowingly!

> Your sister in Christ,
> Lucy

Precious Group,

I bought a garter belt yesterday. You may be saying, "Excuse me, Lucy – you're going to have a reflection on a garter belt? Is nothing sacred?" Well, I've got to tell somebody – Winton's not home – Jud's not interested – so you're the most likely candidates.

I've never had a garter belt before. I went from puberty to pantyhose! This is important – really. The saleslady had to come in the dressing room yesterday to show me how this thing works. I got the giggles and she did, too. It was the same type giggles I had when I was twelve years old and the Easter Bunny, in my basket, gave me a jewelled razor. I giggled and almost died of embarrassment. Of course my older siblings declared it from the roof tops – "Lucy got a razor!" I blushed all day, but goodness, I was happy and proud! I thought, you mean I'm really old enough to have one of these! I thought those jewels glued on the handle made it about the most beautiful thing I had ever seen.

When Winton finally gave me my engagement ring – I said, "Why, this reminds me of my jeweled razor." Not really – but excitement and pride were felt on both days!

So what about the garter belt? Why, at age forty-one, did I think this was an appropriate purchase or a necessary purchase? Well, you see, I'm two-and-one-half pounds away from my goal weight – the weight I'll be carrying for the rest of my life – to the Lord's Glory. I've been covered up most of my life with pounds, sweaters, overblouses, long skirts, boots, hats, gloves – you name it – I've worn it. I've been programmed to think that nice girls don't show much – that includes skin and bones. I've prided myself on always walking by a mirror and only taking a quick glance – never a long gaze. I wouldn't be caught dead combing my hair or putting on lipstick in public. I'd rather have that wind-blown, washed-out look – so no one would possibly think I was vain. No, I was not vain – just prideful.

One thing I've been learning in this new walk of obedience in eating, is that we are God's "Beautiful People." We are to walk in that. I think those old Puritans really did a number on us. They made us think gray and drab is holy. Goodness, what a disservice to our God! I see nothing in His glorious creation that merits that belief. Why, there are peacocks in every created species – vegetable, mineral or animal – peacocks everywhere! But a lot of us play the old Adam and Eve number, "I'm a sinner. I think I'll put on some more pounds and clothes, just to be sure I'm covered." But we are covered! We are covered by the cross!

When you want to read a juicy story, read Solomon's "Song of Songs." This can be seen as a one-on-one love hymn from our Lord God to his beloved – you and me. When you love and know you are loved – you glow – and a garter belt doesn't hurt either!

You sister in Christ,
Glowingly,
Lucy

Precious Group,

I love spend-the-night parties. From age 11 to 18 I attended an all-girls school and one of the most favorite activities was the spend-the-night party. Almost every Friday or Saturday night there would be from 10 to 20 girls that would spend the night together. Although the locations would vary and the houses change, the conversation and menu wouldn't. We shared secrets, clothes, cosmetics and onion dip.

In our pre-driving days, we had "Ma," my friend Amanda's eighty-year-old grandmother, for our chauffeur. She not only knitted each one of us a sweater (mine was green), but she would pick us up after the movie, fill us up with milkshakes and then, to top off a perfect evening, drive us to "Lover's Lane," where we'd honk and giggle. In this wonderful environment, many a heartbreak was mended — many a problem solved — many a tear dried. We learned at an early age how to share each other's pain and problems.

For the past four days I've been on a grown-up spend-the-night party. Winton and I are fortunate to have seven couples that we yearly spend time with together — actually spend-the-night party time. Now that's quality time!

Somehow, when you spend more than forty-eight hours together — morning, noon and night — a depth of conversation is reached like at no other time. When you greet each other in the morning with bathrobes and no make-up — only coffee — you get down to the real nitty gritty of your life. When you do all the daily activities together — ride around in the car together — eat all meals together — and end the day sitting around the fire together — there is an intimacy reached that is glorious.

I'm so glad that Jesus didn't have "nine to five" Disciples. They ate and walked and talked and lived twenty-four hours a day with each other. This type of intimacy is total. They knew our Lord as only a spend-the-night party allows.

Yesterday morning, at our "party," I read **John 19:25a** during my quiet time. I love when a Bible verse comes and lives with me for a day or two. It usually is an unexpected visitor, just popping into my mind and dancing for a little while and then leaving. I read — "But there were standing by the cross of Jesus, His mother and His mother's sister, Mary the wife of Clopas, and Mary Magdalene." **John 19:25b**. It continued to cling to me. I needed to experience the scene for a moment. I felt it had secrets for me to learn — then it could leave, possibly never to return again, but its shared secrets would remain.

"But there were standing by the cross of Jesus, His mother, and His mother's sister, Mary the wife of Clopas, and Mary Magdalene." **John 19:25b**. I've read that verse numerous times in my life, but it never clung to me. Why now? I guess it has to do with where I am today in my life. I understand more deeply how Mother Mary, of course, would stand by her child, share in His suffering, all the while wishing she could totally take it away. I've experienced my four children's hurts, pains and disappointments deeply, wished and prayed that I could be their "stand in," but could only be their "stand by." Especially as they reach maturity, there's more call for standing by than bandaids.

And the friends; I understand those friends of Jesus standing by. How often have I experienced the love of a dear friend who will meet me in my pain – not necessarily saying anything – just "standing by." Oh, the comfort and support it affords. And these friends at this spend-the-night party; there is a lot of "standing by" being done by each one of us as we continue to share our lives.

The men see each other every other month, but as couples, we see each other only annually. Our "standing" has to be so strong, for we only have a few days to share, then we go back to our different cities, our different worlds, but all strengthened. The support will last for another year. It must be how it was when the Disciples were sent out into the world and would then come back together to be renewed, refurbished, rejuvenated, by their Lord and then by the Holy Spirit and each other.

Lent's getting ready to start. It is my prayer this year that I will "stand by" the cross these forty days. In my mind, I've looked at the cross before. In my mind, I've tried to carry one. But I've never for forty days "stood by" – tried to really soak in what was going on – is going on – on that cross. I want to be counted. "All those in favor, please stand." "Oh Lord, I want to kneel, but you want me to stand?"

When we were in our late twenties, Winton and I rented a lake house with his first cousin. One of our prized possessions was a rented jukebox. I loved to play "Stand by Your Man" over and over. This was my theme song. I would sing along louder than the record; why I even had hand motions to go along with this "class act." The point being, I was and am firm in my loyalty to my man. I was and am committed.

For the next forty days I want to be that committed to "The Man" – "The Man Jesus" – my Lord. I want to live at the foot of the cross – so firmly planted that by Good Friday, I'll understand my Lord a little deeper – by Easter, I'll understand my Lord a little deeper – by Ascension, I'll understand my Lord a little deeper – by Pentecost, I'll understand my Lord a little deeper. It is my fervent prayer that because of "standing by," I'll be able to take up my cross and follow Him closer this year.

For Lent, I'm going to a spend-the-night party with the Lord. It's located at the foot of the cross. I believe there will be secrets told. I can't wait! You're invited, too. Please come.

Your sister in Christ,

Lucy

Precious Group,

I went snowmobiling yesterday and it was fantastic! I love Winton so much, because in so many instances he won't take "no" for an answer. You see, I'm basically a chicken. If I had my way, I would probably still be riding a bicycle with training wheels. I like safety and rules – going 55 miles an hour – but Winton makes me stretch my boundaries, my limits.

Yesterday I was stretched by going snowmobiling. Three couples rode on a bus for 45 minutes, out into the snowy wilderness. I had cold feet, not only figuratively, but literally! We were late starting and I wished we would be early stopping! I had on stockings, long underwear, ski pants, two sweaters, ski jacket, gloves, goggles, and then we added helmets, boots and bib overalls. I could barely "moon walk," much less straddle a snowmobile seat. Please, can't I just drink hot chocolate in the warming house or at least ride behind you? No! "Ladies and gentlemen – start your engines." Help! There were eight of us in our party with two guides, one in the front, the other in the back to help. Why didn't he hear me yell, "Help?" Off we went across a huge field. Hey, this is a cinch! Wait a minute – why are we going into the woods on a tiny trail? There are trees on either side of me – we're climbing a mountain – there're no trees on one side, just a cliff! You want me to lean to the left – lean to the right – go team – go team – fight, fight, fight? Help!

Yea, we get to stop! One of the ladies went off the trail and fell off. Great! If I do that can we stop again?

"Ladies and gentlemen, start your engines!" On and on and on we went. Up – down – round – and about, on this narrow little trail. Hey, have you thought about using a bulldozer to widen this thing? Finally we arrive at the meadows. Great! Can we go home now? Is the bus coming to get us? It's getting dark! Don't wolves and coyotes and bears and Indians come out at night? Help!

"You have 15 minutes to ride around in the meadows at full speed, so go have fun!"

You mean we can play chase and try to run into each other at 45 miles an hour? Great! Help! Doesn't anybody care that it's getting dark? Thanks for the hot chocolate and the brownie (I had one bite), but really, I'd rather have the warming house, if you don't mind!

Living on the edge.

Mary Barwick

"Time's up. We go back the same way we came." Isn't there a short-cut? I know the moon is out, but really, it is a little dark. I mean, I can't see! Help!

Each snowmobile had one little dim headlight and two even smaller red tail-lights. We were to stay ten yards from each other and off we went. In the moonlit night, the trees became silvery – the darkness enveloped us and made the boundaries so pronounced. You felt safer in the darkness than in the light. I had one focus – the two little red lights in front of me – up, down, over, around, again. Halfway we stopped, turned off our lights and engines , to soak up the beauty. The snow made the world glow – stars, moon, winter quiet. It was breath-taking – literally and figuratively.

Finally, we arrived safely back. Finally, we got to go in the warming house. The lady of the house was very much pregnant with her fourth child. She was the brownie-maker and you could tell, an earth mother. In this totally isolated world, she had brought warmth to a home. A wood fire was burning in a stove and a little stained-glass church was hanging in the window.

The picture that popped into my mind was the wonderful painting of Christ standing in the dark of the night, holding a lantern which illuminates part of His face. He's showing me the way – drawing me to Him. You can't see anything to the right or to the left – dark, just like it was in the woods; but a safe dark, a limiting, boundaried dark – which makes it imperative to follow the light – the Light.

The snowmobile, with its single light, brought me to this safe haven – a house with a little stained-glass church hanging in the window. My Lord is bringing me to a safe haven – a home – His Light shows me the Way.

"Ladies and gentlemen, start your engines!"

Your sister in Christ,

Lucy

Precious Group,

I'm going deep today if you don't mind. You see, my daddy died thirteen years ago today – oh, and did I love my daddy and he loved me. I miss him. It makes me sad that my children only have a slight memory of him. He was wonderful. He did everything 100%, worked, played, loved – 100%. It is because of his unconditional love that it has always been very easy for me to understand my Lord God's love. Of course, Jesus called his Father "Abba" = Daddy, for he experienced that 100% love, too.

In my most favorite picture of Daddy and me, he's seated and I have my head in his lap, sucking my thumb. I must have been about six years old. The picture symbolizes Daddy's kind of love. I remember overhearing my grandparents talking about how awful it was that I sucked my thumb. I remember having some horrible, ucky stuff, painted on my thumb so I wouldn't suck it. It was a complete embarrassment to everyone, except Daddy. In the picture, he has his arms around me, with a smile on his face.

That is the picture I continue to carry in my mind. A father loving his child unconditionally. That is also the picture I carry of my Lord God. I don't know why He called me into being. I know I must constantly be a disappointment to Him, not living up to His mark, His expectations – but He loves me. He loves me – Lucy. He loves you!

Today is the most fantastically beautiful day that you can imagine. We awakened to sixteen inches of new snow. The drive to the airport was breathtaking – the mountains, meadows, and trees blanketed in this white shimmering sparkle. A blue, blue sky – unbelievable. The view from the airplane was also magnificent. All you could see were snow-covered mountains, clouds, and blue, blue sky.

It reminded me of "Buddy's Run." "Buddy's Run" is the name of the upper-most ski trail at Steamboat Springs, Colorado. It was named for Buddy Werner, a member of the U.S. Olympic Ski Team in the Fifties. He was killed in an avalanche in Switzerland. I had seen his picture earlier – handsome, athletic, full of life, full of potential. How tragic, I thought – and then I saw "Buddy's Run" and the tragedy had been turned into a triumph. I cannot tell you the awesomeness of the view – more glorious than any cathedral that I have ever seen. It took my breath away. It was very steep and the mountain view went forever. You felt like if you weren't weighed down, you could just take right off into heaven – right into Buddy's world – right into Daddy's world – right into God's everlasting arms.

I love Paul's declaring for all eternity, "For I am persuaded, that neither death, nor life, nor angels, nor principalities, nor powers, nor things present, nor things to come, nor height, nor depth, nor any other creature, shall be able to separate us from the love of God, which is in Christ Jesus our Lord." **Romans 8:38-39**. I also am persuaded.

I love my Lord Jesus saying, "Let not your heart be troubled: ye believe in God, believe also in me. In my Father's house are many mansions: if it were not so, I would have told you. I go to prepare a place for you. And if I go and prepare a place for you, I will come again, and receive you unto myself; that where I am, there ye may be also. And whether I go ye know, and the way ye know." **John 14:1-4**.

I had a Daddy who unconditionally loved me; in fact, that "had" needs to be changed to "have," for that type of love doesn't end. I have the Father God who unconditionally loves me.

He sent His Son just to be sure that I'd make it back to Him.

I believe the "worlds" are closer than we can even imagine – only a breath away. The view from "Buddy's Run" felt eternal – you could almost picture going from the finite to the infinite. The view from my airplane window has the same feeling. The awesomeness of God surrounds me – as I am sure it surrounds my daddy and Buddy and His other Saints. My God, I thank you for the views – and for Daddy.

Your sister in Christ,

Lucy

Precious Group,

I saw a picture of God yesterday. He looked just the way I had expected.

For Valentine's, I gave Mary Barwick letters twelve through twenty-eight. I delivered them in a big pink plastic envelope, with a white doily heart pasted on the outside. I was so excited! I couldn't wait to ring the door, smile and say "here" – but she wasn't home! Oh, what a letdown – 8:30 in the morning and Mary wasn't home! I was so surprised because every time I'd had a delivery before – she not only was home, but usually walking out the door to greet me.

You see, we have been having a joy walk together and usually things just happen. I first ran into Mary about three weeks before Christmas. I had received a card from Katie, at the bookstore, that "The Alabama Angels" had arrived. I didn't know what that meant, but I did and do know about angels; in fact, I collect them, just to remind me of their constant near-ness. Katie knew my love and for years had been recommending wonderful books for me. I had never been led astray – so if Katie said "The Alabama Angels" were arriving – I knew I needed to be there to greet them. You know, Santa arrives at the Mall a day after Thanksgiving so it made perfect sense to me that "The Alabama Angels" would zoom in three weeks before Christmas. I also knew Handel's "Hallelujah Chorus," if they needed an extra singer. I arrived at the store – but there was no Katie – no angels flying – only a thin little paperback lying on the counter. In a pitiful, disappointed little voice, I said, "Oh, is this 'The Alabama Angels'?" – gulp – trying to keep my composure and not show my disappointment. "I'll take one, please." I walked dejectedly back to my red Blazer and took a courtesy glance at my purchase – then read it – laughed at it – rejoiced for it and ran back and bought thirty more copies.

In five minutes my Christmas shopping had been completed. Now, with time on my hands, I asked the saleslady if she possibly had Mary Barwick's telephone number, because I wanted to call her and let her know that I was in love. I went to a phone booth and called. Of course,

Mary was at home – of course, only lived a few blocks away and of course, would love for me to visit. She asked, "When?" I said "Now!" It was love at first sight – a soulmate! Yea!

(I add all of these "of courses" because our encounters, our conversations, our dreams have always been so in tune.)

A few weeks later, I was driving home from the lake on a beautiful Sunday afternoon. The idea formed in my mind to make a book out of the weekly letters that I'd been writing my study group. Lucy, how many letters? Fifty-two. One for each week of the year. But I can't spell and my grammar is terrible. Well then, don't you think humorous paintings would go perfectly with your style? I wish precious Lida Holly was alive. How about her friend, the Angel Lady?

The next day I thought, Lucy, that was a harebrained idea, probably too much caffeine, but just in case, you could go by Mary's house. I could remember the street, so I turned down it. I thought, Lord this is crazy! I'm crazy! I don't remember which house is hers or her last name. Am I just going to ride around or go play "Trick or Treat" in December, until I find her? Down the road I went – yellow. Lucy, remember, the house was your favorite color – yellow. But which yellow? Pale yellow? Bright yellow? "Help!" As I drove, out walked Mary. I told her my idea – told her when twelve letters were written, I'd bring them to her. We talked about Lida and the Lord. We laughed and talked fast and she didn't think I was crazy. Her book and paintings had been created in the same manner. Divine dictation might be too strong for the public. Divine inspiration might be too strong for the public. All Mary and I knew was that we were getting a whole lot of "Help" and it wasn't from our publishers!

A few weeks later, with twelve letters in hand, I drove back to Mary's. Of course, she was home. A few weeks later – with sixteen letters in hand – I drove back to Mary's. Of course, she wasn't at home! I left them anyway. Doubt crept into my mind. Maybe twenty-eight letters were all I was supposed to write. Maybe there's no book. Maybe the letters were for Mama's birthday. Maybe so I could practice my penmanship and improve my spelling. Maybe… and then the phone rang. It was Mary. Her beautiful voice said, "I have completed two paintings for the book, can you come see them?" – Gulp – the dream lived once more!

The paintings were wonderful, just as I had imagined. One had a rose, the other had a rainbow. I knew which letter went with the rose, but "Mary, tell me about the rainbow. Which letter does it portray?" She saw it as the cover. Oh, the dream not only lives, but had a cover now! I floated out her front door and Mary called me back to come see something special. We went into her kitchen and there she showed me some of her fan mail from a grammar school.

"Lucy, I thought you'd like to see this. It's a picture of God." And sure enough – there He was. A triangle for His body and two outstretched triangles for his arms. He had a big smile and GOD written on His chest, just to be sure you knew who He was – I did.

And I do and you do too! We just need to be more in tune – more of a listener – quieter – more focused – more anticipative. My best prayer is "Lord, it's me, Lucy. I'm here." and really be "here." He meets me every time. He is faithful about keeping His appointment. We just have to be faithful in keeping our appointment with Him. Of course, He's always at home and if we allow Him, He'll show us His picture, too.

"Now Lord, how did you actually get that triangular shape of yours? Does it have any significance or symbolism?"

Your sister in Christ,

Lucy

Precious Group,

I saw two prisons yesterday. Although the first was just a replica, it was the most oppressive space that I have ever experienced. It was located at Gunter Air Station in their "Air Force Enlisted Men's Museum" and depicted a North Vietnamese prison cell. The space was about eight feet by four feet. There were roaches on the wall, a wooden cot, a refuse bucket. They had allowed visiting ex-POW's to autograph the walls. It was a despicable place! I wanted to give a bloody scream at the inhumanity! Over the years, I've had the privilege of hearing three different POW's tell their story. Each had stuck a barb deep into my heart – and this eight-foot-by-four-foot space brought their stories to life. You could almost smell the filth – the heat – the humiliation – the oppression.

After this, we went to Maxwell Air Force Minimum Security Prison. I had always heard that it was like a country club. True, it was nice – new buildings, good food, tennis courts, exercise facilities, no cells but dorms – but it definitely was a prison. I saw no joy in the faces of these green-clothed men. They were allowed to walk freely around the facility, but that freedom was limited. They were bound, not shackled like the POW's, but never-the-less bound – limited, restrained. Their freedom was gone. You could see it in their eyes and in their posture.

Some days, I feel like we have those same eyes – that same posture. The prison walls are our own making, built by our own unconfessed sins. We use slimy fears and doubts for mortar. Pride and self-centered actions are our furnishings. The rotting smell is similar to the POW's world.

Why, O Lord my God – why do we imprison ourselves from you? But, thank you Lord – you continually rain Your grace upon us, causing the mortar to wash away and the walls to crumble down. The shackles fall away. Your grace brings confession, brokenness, and freedom. Isn't it a paradox that with our total surrender – our total brokenness – comes total freedom. But how often is God's way diametrically opposed to this "world's" way?

"You want freedom – surrender completely – then I'll give you freedom."

In three of the Gospels it says "Jesus was bound." **Matthew 27:2a, Mark 15:1b, John 18:12b.** It was this binding – this surrendering to the cross that allowed His eternal victory – our eternal freedom.

My mind dwells on the man who lived in the tombs (**Mark 5:2-20**). Tombs – how awful! An unholy place for the Jew. A place of decay and death. A leper was avoided physically, but this "tomb dweller" would have had it even worse – totally ostracized, despised and hated. It says "he had often been bound with shackles and chains." And then Jesus came – sent his demons into the swine. His walls were knocked down – he was healed – made whole – set free.

Have you had "tomb dwelling" days? Built your own prisons or sepulchers? The good news – I mean really "Good News" – people – is that the "Grace Rain" causes floods daily and those old walls won't stand – they'll just be washed away – in the blood of the Lamb. **Revelations 12:11, I Peter 1:18-19.**

> Your sister in Christ,
> Lucy

Precious Group,

"Lights – Camera – Action." Today I want to write about light – "prism" light. Lucy, there's no such word. Well, then – let's make it up! What I'm talking about is the glorious miracle that occurs when light travels through a prism and breaks forth into a glorious rainbow of color. I remember my grammar school science lesson on prisms and how they work. If I edited that text, I would insist that the word "miracle" be added.

Today in this twentieth-century world, we proceed to explain away the miraculous – like rainbows. Thank goodness, we'll always have the inquisitive wisdom of three-year-olds who are forever asking "why." "Why" on every subject – and not just one "why," but numerous "whys" until the exasperated adult finally answers, "Because I said so!"

I propose that a better answer would be, "It's a miracle." I bet then the "whys" would cease more quickly – with a "Wow!" or an "Oh." (Inferring, "Why didn't you say that in the first place, Dummy?")

I'd have to respond with, "Wise child," for they really are. "How did you know my name was Dummy?" I've tried to hide that name with big answers! Your "whys" make me dig and dig and dig – back to the source. I mean "The Source" – our Creator God – who reigns at the center of all of our questions. You know, I bet that those three-year-old wisemen instinctively know the answers and were placed on this earth to continually remind us of "the Fact" – of "The Source" – Thank you, Lord, for the miracle of three-year-olds.

The miracle that I'd like to focus on today, however, is "prism light." I love the stained glass Ascension window over the altar at our church. It is a beautiful representation of my Lord's "lift off" in glorious living color. Sunday it was more glorious than usual, because the wall next to the window was ablaze in reflected color. Another dance of light was created on the wall – brighter than the original.

The same phenomenon occurred that afternoon at a wedding. The huge side blue window was haloed by a rainbow. Glorious. Each window was a good example of man's best effort of beauty. They had taken months to create – and then in a second, a minute, a moment, their beauty was paled by a flash of God's light. I mean – an instant "wallflower" created!

Another "light dance" comes to mind. Winton and I were informed that our home's original dining room chandelier was available. It had been stored about fifteen years in an old warehouse. We weren't expecting much more than a gargoyled monster of a light – strictly Victorian. Out of courtesy, we felt that a viewing was necessary.

We walked to the back of the dimly lit building and there it hung – beauty. Instead of an oppressive Victorian monster it was a grand old prismed jewel – just waiting to be set aglow once more. "Lights – Camera – Action." Yea! With the electricity flowing once more – her dance continued – no – continues!

You know, you can take an ordinary old piece of crystal, give it some facets, shine light through it and glittering rainbows appear. I believe that life has that same effect on us. We mostly enter this world blemish-free and then, with time – with living – facets begin to appear. Our real character comes forth. As Christians – our real character – the shine which comes forth – is Christ's. His light is there at the very instant that we proclaim Him as our Lord and our Savior. All during our lives, we continue to acquire new facets – new brokenness – which allows His Light to shine through us. The indwelling of the Holy Spirit affords such a powerful wattage – such an infinite "Power Source."

"Why?" "Miracle – my three-year-old wise child – Miracle." "Oh!"

One of the popular songs in the musical Annie is "It's a Hard-Knock Life." A lot of us go around with this mindset. As Christians, don't you think "multi-faceted" might be a better way for us to approach the fine tuning that life affords?

I don't know why "Lights, Camera, Action" keeps blasting into my brain. All I know is that there is a glorious dance going on — there are no "wallflowers" — just miracles — a "rainbow dance."

How are your facets coming along?

Are they reflecting "the Light"?

Your sister in Christ,

Lucy

Precious Group,

I love babies. They are the ultimate surprise package. Last week I had the joy of experiencing two blessed baby happenings. The first was at the hospital, waiting for my new nephew to be born. It was so much fun! I haven't done that in a long time and I had forgotten that unique pleasure, the sheer delight!

Besides our party of five, there were twenty others. Previously strangers, we became bonded by birthings. We had four babies born during our four hour wait. It was thrilling! The father would come in and tell the family the good news. We all would rejoice. Everyone told old birthing stories, which in my mind, are a lot more interesting than old football ones! We giggled and laughed and congratulated one another.

When there was a lull in the activity, we'd all walk down to the nursery and look at the new arrivals. What a view! Twenty babies, eighteen boys and two girls, all lined up, all wrapped in blue and pink swaddling clothes. They were gorgeous! "Stunning!" (That's Winton's new word and I'm borrowing it, for "stunning" is just right for that moment.) For to look upon that many miracles at one time did leave you "stunned!" The party atmosphere of the waiting room would give way to a reverent quiet. I wished I had brought a little gold, frankincense, and myrrh to pass out — for holiness was there. God's presence seemed very close.

In Genesis, I love how each Creation Day ended with the declaration — "And it was good." That same creative goodness permeated the Nursery. Of course, the real world would soon come crashing in — sin would soon invade those precious babies' world, because of their humanity. But at that moment, that brief moment — their God origin seemed to be still clinging to them. "Stunning!"

The other blessed baby moment was at church. We had a Baptism and I love Baptisms! They are always festive, with the whole congregation getting into the act. In our church, it is the custom for the baby to be brought forth and presented by his parents and godparents. Vows are taken by all present to nurture this new baby Christian.

Then a wonderful Recessional to the font, at the back of the church, takes place. It resembles more a festival parade rather than a stately march. Behind the Baptismal party, fall in all the children of the church. There is a "Pied Piper" type atmosphere — some run, some walk, others are coaxed, until all gather at the Baptismal Font. The baby is baptized by the minister and then the "Parade" begins again. We then "welcome the newly baptized into the household of faith." It is a wonderful sacrament and celebration.

Naturally, the center of attraction is the baby. Being in the choir, I have the benefit of seeing everything up close. Usually the sopranos, like fairy godmothers, look down and quietly "ooh and aaah" over the preciousness of the baby, but Sunday was different. For me, the mother outshone her child. Now I don't mean to down-play the baby, he was beautiful — but the mother shined — for she cried.

In all my years of baptismal experiences, this was a first and it touched me deeply. It reminded me of all of the mothers in the Old Testament who would bring their first-born sons to the Temple to be dedicated to God. Although this became a ceremonial gift, the symbolism spoke loudly. They acknowledged to all the sacred gift of a child given to them by their Creator God. It is an awesome responsibility!

This young mother, with tears flowing, seemed to comprehend that timeless responsibility and the Godliness of the gift. Our silence in the Nursery also acknowledged the holy mystery. Our Creator God was at work once more. "And it was good!" The age-old "Creation Proclamation" seems to continue to reverberate across the ages, continues to be stated — by mothers — by fathers — by families — by congregations — "And It Was Good!" — "And It Was Good!" — "And It Was Good!" — Amen.

Your sister in Christ,

Lucy

G'day Mates,

I'm "down under" in the wonderful city of Sydney, Australia. And that's what I'd like to write about to you — the "down under" of my world — or the "topsy-turvy" of my world. What amazes me is that you put me on a plane for thirty hours, mess with my eating and sleeping habits and the result is not a happy camper!

I'm right now getting ready to call up room service and ask them to please remove their completely stocked little refrigerator, for it is no longer completely stocked. In the past two days I've had health food — consisting mainly of nuts and fruit, until they've become unhealthy. I've had juices, coffee, tea, diet cokes, and the straw that broke the camel's back was two granola bars covered with chocolate. "Help! Room service – get this thing out of here! I mean pull it out of the wall!" I've become like the plant in *The Little Shop of Horrors* – "Feed Me!" – but I'm not hungry – I'm tired. My metabolic clock has gone haywire, been turned upside down.

I'm expected to sit in classes all day long and take comprehensive, intelligent, precise notes, when my body clock keeps saying "Bedtime, Lucy!" Each night at dinner time, I'm supposed to be charming and vivacious, with direct eye contact and visible interest shown to one thousand of my new-found international friends. I can't even focus on what they're saying – much less their eyes.

This jet-lag affliction has really taught me something about myself. Much to my great disappointment, I've come to the realization that I'm not astronaut material. I can live with this short-coming, but I'm not quite so sure of another one.

You know in **Matthew 26:36-41** it recounts a very personal, intimate story of "Four Mates," as the Aussies would say, and one of them is really having a rough go of it – in fact, His life is on the line. All He asks of His mates is that they will stand by Him. He says, "My soul is deeply grieved to the point of death, remain here and keep watch with Me." He's not asking them to share in His grief or death – just to stand – to support – to be present. The old Lucy would jump at the chance, for I have a little Florence Nightingale, "Flying Nun," in me – but now, after this acute bout of jet lag, I'd have to truthfully say, "Excuse me, is that Central Standard Time or Aussie time that you'll be needing me?"

It says that after praying, Jesus returned to His best friends, His closest mates in the world – the ones He thought He could count on – He found them sleeping. He said, "So, you men could not watch with Me for one hour? Keep watching and praying, that you may not enter into temptation. The spirit is willing, but the flesh is weak."

You know, my Lord could have just as easily been addressing Lucy as Peter, James and John. Right now I'm wearing my pretty little fourteen-karat gold cross around my neck. I'm carrying my little blue New Testament in my purse, ready to pull it out at a moment's notice. Next to our hotel bed, lugged all the way from Alabama to Sydney, is my New American Standard Bible with concordance and my favorite devotional books. I mean, I'm a "marching army for the Lord" – if I've had my sleep. Lucy – "the spirit is willing, but the flesh is weak." Yes, Lord, but I thought that at any time or place, at the drop of a hat, I could stand up and be counted for You. Lucy, "the spirit is willing, but the flesh is weak."

I guess it's about time that I really understand that statement. I mean, really comprehend my weaknesses and limitations. I know I've read those passages numerous times, but deep inside, I've pridefully thought, "You know good and well, Lucy Blount, if you set your mind to it, you could do anything!" No You Can't. Lucy, you think jet lag is bad, I guarantee there will be a few more "life rides" that are going to be "loop-the-loops" and it's going to be the spirit – I mean "the Spirit" – "His Spirit" that allows you to witness in the hard times – the "out-of-whack" times.

I think of the saints and martyrs of the past and those living today. I believe they've all been and are ordinary people, for we've all been from the beginning just "dust stuff." The difference is the spirit propulsion, I mean "Spirit Propulsion." There's no jet lag, no cold feet, no ambiguity with the "Energizer."

In John's beautifully loving Gospel, he simply stated after his Christ's resurrection, (**John 20:19b-22**) "Jesus came and stood in their midst, and said to them, 'Peace be with you.' And when He had said this, He showed them both His hands and His side. The disciples therefore rejoiced when they saw the Lord. Jesus therefore said to them again, 'Peace be with you; as the Father has sent Me, I also send you.' And when He had said this, He breathed on them and said to them 'Receive the Holy Spirit.'" The Healer – the Comforter – the Gift Giver – the Guide – the Illuminator – the Revealer – the Teacher – the Helper – the Sanctifier – the Empowerer.

That's dynamic news! It is Christ's Spirit in us that does not allow mountains to be made out of mole hills. He knows of the stuff we're made and it's not "tough stuff" or "hot stuff," just dust – but with a little bit of breath – His breath – ah – the Saints begin to activate and it doesn't matter a "hill of beans" what the Greenwich Mean Time is!

> Breathe on me, Breath of God, fill me with life anew,
>   That I may love what thou dost love, and do what thou wouldst do.
> Breathe on me, Breath of God, until my heart is pure,
>   Until with thee I will one will, to do or to endure.
> Breathe on me, Breath of God, till I am wholly thine,
>   'Till all this earthly part of me glows with thy fire divine.
> Breathe on me, Breath of God, so shall I never die;
>   But live with thee the perfect life of thine eternity.[1]

Your sister in Christ,
Lucy

[1] The Hymnal 1982: Hymn #508
Edwin Hatch (1835-1889)

Precious Group,

"Where my lack of love might have limited Yours – Lord, forgive."

I understand the concept of turning the other cheek. I've even practiced this maneuver a couple of times – that's me, dealing with a personal hurt, one inflicted personally to me alone and no one else and I understand that. I can swivel the head back and forth for the blow pretty easily.

The one I'm having the hardest time comprehending – the one that gets stuck in my craw – the one that I can't seem to swallow, or sometimes when I think finally it's gone, the gnawing stopped – it unexpectedly resurfaces again – is how do you turn the other cheek when the one who was hurt is not you, but one you love? Boy, there's a difference and boy, it's hard!

I'm a mother. I'm made to kiss it and make it better – but what do you do when you can't – when you can't take the other's pain away?

I love the old movie "Dirty Harry" where Clint Eastwood tells the bad guy to draw his gun – "Come on, make my day!" – and he blows him away – "Bang, you're dead!" And that's the way our VCR world works – "Bang, you're dead." – instant justification – instant gratification – instant solution to the problem – but that's not the real world. And thank the dear Lord it isn't, for our world deserves the "big bang" daily – but doesn't get it.

When I lose my perspective, my Christ–centered orientation, I find myself wanting to stand on a soap box and shout, with clinched fists, "But God, this isn't right!"

I seem to hear in response, "Lucy, it hasn't been right since sin slithered in."

"But Lord, let me tell you about this injustice. I'm sure you'll want to do something about it – just a little zapping – please. I mean it's really bad!"

I seem to hear – "Lucy, I've already done something about it – I gave my Son – my only Son – my sinless Son – to you, the sinful."

"Oh Lord, forgive."

I seem to hear – "I already have."

"Then Lord, what am I to do? It hurts so bad! I think I've forgiven. I think I'm making a little headway, being a little bit more Christian in my outlook – and then, "Wham!" – that putrid taste comes back – that anger hardens my heart once more. I'm so tired of it! I want to let it go, but I seem not to be able. I keep looking at the old situation – keep playing the old tapes – picking at the wound until it festers once more. There are always the same "good guys" and the same "bad guys" – but it never ends, at least, not to my liking.

So what Lord, do You want me to do? Would you like me to reverse the roles? Make the "good guys" bad and "bad guys" good? But Lord, that's ridiculous! It's not fair – not how you play the game!

I seem to hear "It's the way I play the game – remember My Son's innocent death?"

So in my mind, I recast the stuck scene and guess who gets to wear black? And that's not my most becoming color! There's only one line that I've had to learn, thus far, in this new version. I don't know how it's going to come out, how the last scene is played – but on second thought – maybe I do – I think it takes place on Calvary.

My line goes, "Where my lack of love might have limited Yours – Lord, forgive."

Lucy, say it once more, with deep feeling and humility – "Where my lack of love might have limited Yours – Lord, forgive."

Lucy, once more – deeper, more humble, with a broken heart – "Where my lack of love might have limited Yours – Lord, forgive."

It's just a cameo part. I wear black. Thus far, I have only one line, but it seems to be the key to the plot. The plot doesn't seem to thicken now, in fact, it seems to be more flowing. I'm not called to "kiss and make it better" in this new role. I'm called to have brokenness, so that the real "Star," the "Healer," can begin to work.

Do you have some stuck "starring" roles in your life, that need to be freed up? Try recasting them. Cameo parts have won many an actor an Oscar, or maybe even better, a "well done, good and faithful servant."

Your sister "starlet" in Christ,
Lucy

Hello Luv,

I just climbed the Sydney Harbour Bridge. This was a big deal! In the fifty-eight years of its existence, they had never let a group do this. Only safety inspectors and repair crews were allowed up to this 440-foot-high top chord of the bridge. The first thing you had to do was sign a liability waiver – then you climbed single-file up two vertical steel ladders to a four-foot-wide curved walkway which you followed to the top.

Why? Why would I do such a crazy thing? I just finished being furious at my middle son for jumping off a 125-foot bridge with only a bungee cord connected to his ankles. And here I am 440 feet above the water, walking on top of a bridge, on a four-foot-wide ladder with nothing connected to my ankles, just tennis shoes. I've lost all my credibility for being called a "chicken." Why?

It started raining and blowing right when we reached the top. Our guide piled all seven of our group into the crane house. Smiling, with a wild glint in his eyes, it was obvious that he'd been at it for over twenty years. The weather got so bad that another group joined us — fourteen in all — in a space made for one crane operator! All the other tours were cancelled and here we were, packed like sardines, in a tin room — wind and rain howling and blowing all around. Our guide recounted how many people had died during construction, maintenance, and suicide jumps. I couldn't decide whether he was a descendant of Captain Cook, the founder of Sydney, or of Captain Hook. I mean the whole experience was bizarre! The view was magnificent, when you could see, and the fear was real. But why? I still don't know. It was too close to the edge of my comfort zone, for I am not the frontier, pioneer type!

The theme for this conference was "Managing New Frontiers." I need to tell someone that I would like a remedial course. I can't even manage the old frontiers, much less the new ones. I guess they haven't heard about my closets and drawers, or know of my scheduling and organizing skills. I'll just keep smiling and taking notes and holding on for dear life!

I wanted to tell my "bridge group" that they could see the same view, with exactly the same weather conditions, it they took the elevator up to the thirty-first floor of our hotel. For you see, I'd done that the day before. There I sat, for three hours, looking out the window, as two Japanese men swam laps. I'm sure they thought, "Crazy American woman, sitting in her hot black knit jump suit, in this steamy room," — for I thought, "Crazy Japanese men, swimming in their tiny little black knit swim suits." Anyway, I liked sitting there a lot.

The alternative had been to go flying with Winton to a sheep ranch forty-five minutes away. And I'd come really close to going. I took the bus out to the airport — was continuing even when they said only one of two airplanes would be able to fly because of mechanical problems — was continuing even when, buckled in, they said we would have to wait for an hour until the weather got better — was continuing. Hold it! I want off! No more new frontiers today for me, please. Quietly I got up, kissed Winton good-bye, deplaned and went to the swimming pool room at the top of the hotel. I don't know why it wasn't featured in the Guide Book — "Glorious view" — "Controlled environment" — "Reasonably priced refreshments" (a Coke machine right around the corner).

"Managing New Frontiers" — what a provocative, presumptuous theme! But who's the manager? I wish I had one of those little booths like they have at airports where "unusuals" do their hawking at the passers-by. I'd set up right in the middle of the conference center and hand out opened Gideons that I would have collected from their hotel rooms. "G'day Mates — Hello Luv, get your free copy of this here best seller! Learn how to be a better manager by 'the

Manager' and speaking of new frontiers – forget it! He's already not only conquered them, but He created them! So, sit back, slow down, relax, have yourself a cool drink in the shade and do a little Good Book reading. It's action-packed, with a lot of take-home value. I bet it will receive a ten on your evaluation sheet."

I bet I'd really be good at this, truly convincing, with great sincerity because the only thing I've learned in this life, thus far – I mean, that I am really sure of – is that each day is a gift – a new frontier – uniquely different from any other, even if the routine and the schedule looks identically the same – it won't be. And the other fact that I am absolutely sure of is that I can't manage it. I can play like I can, even fool myself and others, for a while – but I'm not the manager – the CEO – the President – the ruler – my Master is.

And ah ha! I knew it! The conference planners do know who the real "Manager" is after all! Even though they haven't made a verbal declaration of it – they have made a boisterous visual one. For the meeting's logo is a silhouette of the Opera House on the left and the Harbour Bridge on the right. And we have "done" – have "managed" both of these marvelous "man-made" structures. But guess what shines and reigns over both of these structures? Right slap in the middle of the logo hangs the Southern Cross! And guess who's the Manager – the CEO – the President of this glorious sight in the sky?

I received a button for climbing the Harbour Bridge. It says, "I'm an Arch hero." I received a program for attending "La Traviata" at the Opera House. I wonder if tomorrow I'll get a book marker that says, "I Knelt and Gazed at the Southern Cross."

Lord my God – I thank you that all of our "New Frontiers" have already been created, explored and conquered by You. We're under Your constant management, if only we allow – we surrender – we let go –

Psalm 139

1   O Lord, Thou hast searched me and know me.
2   Thou dost know when I sit down and when I rise up; Thou dost understand my thought from afar.
3   Thou dost scrutinize my path and my lying down, and art intimately acquainted with all my ways.
4   Even before there is a word on my tongue, Behold, O Lord, Thou dost know it all.
5   Thou hast enclosed me behind and before, and laid Thy hand upon me.
6   Such knowledge is too wonderful for me; It is too high, I cannot attain to it.
7   Where can I go from Thy Spirit? Or where can I flee from Thy presence?
8   If I ascend to Heaven, Thou art there; If I make my bed in Sheol, behold, Thou art there.
9   If I take the wings of the dawn, If I dwell in the remotest part of the sea,
10 Even there Thy hand will lead me, and thy right hand will lay hold of me.
11 If I say, surely the darkness will overwhelm me, and the light around me will be night,

12   Even the darkness is not dark to Thee, and the night is as bright as the day.
      Darkness and light are alike to Thee.

13   For Thou didst form my inward parts; Thou didst weave me in my mother's womb.

14   I will give thanks to Thee, for I am fearfully and wonderfully made; Wonderful are Thy works,
      And my soul knows it very well.

15   My frame was not hidden from Thee, When I was made in secret, and skillfully wrought
      in the depths of the earth.

16   Thine eyes have seen my unformed substance; and in Thy book they were all written,
      The days that were ordained for me, When as yet there was not one of them.

17   How precious also are Thy thoughts to me, O God! How vast is the sum of them!

18   If I should count them, they would out-number the sand. When I awake, I am still with Thee.

19   O that Thou wouldst slay the wicked, O God; Depart from me, therefore, men of bloodshed.

20   For they speak against Thee wickedly, and Thine enemies take Thy name in vain.

21   Do I not hate those who hate Thee, O Lord? And do I not loathe those who rise up against Thee?

22   I hate them with the utmost hatred; They have become my enemies.

23   Search me, O God, and know my heart; Try me and know my anxious thoughts;

24   And see if there be any hurtful way in me, and lead me in the everlasting way.

      Amen!

I'm going to make an announcement. "Due to New Management, this conference is officially closed!" G'day Mates. Who's managing your frontiers?

Love and Kisses,

Your sister in Christ,

Lucy

Precious Group,

One of my favorite children's book is *The Bears' Vacation*. It is a "Bear" version of the "People" movie version, starring Chevy Chase. Both in the Berenstain book and in the "Vacation" movie, the hero, in a wonderfully wacky sort of way, is "Papa Bear." He has an A-type personality — is a leader — always first in line — is the ruler of his roost. He has a "sort of" willing-to-follow type family. There is no question who is the boss. The route that he takes is usually the most fun one, with some zany detours on the way. He's humored by the group, even if he does wake you up too early and keep you out too late — for you know you'll arrive at your destination — eventually.

I'm married to one of those "Papa Bear" types and those crazy vacations are real and do occur. My children call him the "Dancing Bear" because one of his pleasures in life is to come barrelling into their rooms and pounce on the beds to wake them up. The later they've stayed up, the harder the pounce. They've locked doors, taken phones off the hooks, built barricades —

but to no avail. It's always a losing battle and the sooner they surrender, the fewer the pounces and tickles inflicted.

On this vacation, the troops are down to a bare minimum – me and "the Bear" – and at 4:30 a.m. this morning, how I wished for my back-up battalion. "Wake up! Let's go for a walk and watch the sun come up!"

"But I've only been asleep for four hours and it's dark." I knew there was no out-maneuvering – the attack was on and the sooner the surrender, the sooner I could possibly get back to bed. Besides, you know how I'm a sucker for sunrises and this was our last day in Sydney, so the offer wasn't all bad.

We dressed quickly and hit the streets by 5:00 a.m. to watch the dark turn to day. It was beautiful! The stars and moon slowly faded into the pale sky. The Opera House, the Harbour Bridge, the bay, the birds – unbelievable! I just sat and watched patiently, while "the Bear" roamed from locked gate to locked gate of the Botanical Garden. He was determined to get in. I sat and watched the world as "the Bear" wandered curiously. "Ah ha! Success! An unlocked gate!" – "But let's just sit and watch this wonderful sunrise service."

"Come on!" And off I go, following him into this unknown world. It was fantastic! Trees and bushes and plants and flowers and birds the likes of which I'd never seen. I felt like "Alice in Wonderland," running from one exotic specimen plant to the next. Saying "What is your name?" They were all new and strange to me. "Tell me, what is your name? I want to know you. I want to understand you. I want to comprehend your world. Tell me, what is your name?" And I would read out loud the little brass plaque that each wore.

From this experience, it became even clearer to me why Moses, when first encountering God, asked, "What is your name?" All week long I've worn a little plastic plaque like the plants – "Lucy Blount – Rebel Chapter." People have come up and read my label. The more time that they spent with me and the more time that I spent with them – the more we learned each other's real name and each others real identity.

It's like that, don't you think? "And Moses asked God His name." **Exodus 3:13-14.** That wasn't a one-time encounter – "Two ships passing in the night." Moses learned God's name – "I AM" – and then spent the rest of his life getting to know his God better. I thirst for that knowledge. As His saints, we are to thirst and yearn and spend quality and quantity time with our Lord God.

Jesus says, "Ask and it shall be given to you; seek and ye shall find; knock and it shall be

Winton, the Dancing Bear.

Mary Barwick

opened to you. For everyone who asks receives, and he who seeks finds and to him who knocks it shall be opened." **Matthew 7:7-8.**

This takes time don't you think?

I wish my name tag had not only read "Lucy Blount – Rebel Chapter," but had also printed on it Paul's label, "By the grace of God I am what I am." **I Corinthians 15:10.**

And your name, please?

Your sister in Christ,

Lucy

Precious Group,

"Like streams of living water, my soul thirsts for You."

All my life I've enjoyed streams. As a child, we would play in the stream right behind our house. It was a constant delight. We were lucky enough to have land with hills and woods and lots of children with whom to share adventures. There was a long list of places where we couldn't go and things we could not do – but somehow, amazingly, the stream was always on the allowed list.

Obviously the grown-up world didn't know about the dangerous possibilities of our stream. It could be a moat, protecting a fair damsel from a barbarian attack. It could be a boat launch for great paper ships. Cowboys and Indians and Billy Goat Gruff could invade by way of the stream. Tadpoles and frogs were constantly captured. You could push your enemy into the water or you could splash your friend. If you became exhausted from this strenuous make-believe world, you could just lie down and pick violets or tiny little blue flowers to take home to your doll house.

It's funny now, looking back, that we weren't allowed to play in the fish pond in our garden. Big deal! It was about eight-feet-by-four-feet and two-feet deep, with stagnant water and huge goldfish and lily pads – it was boring. Who would want to get into that smelly old place? But we'd all say, "Yes Ma'am, we promise," look greatly disappointed and then run to the stream – the "living stream," for it was constantly changing. After spring rains, we thought it was a giant river which must be dammed, for the welfare of all. In the hot summer, it would almost dry up and become a grand mud maker, damp enough for our manufacturing of clay ashtrays and delicious mud cakes.

As an adult, this "stream dreaming" continued by way of my children. In Montgomery and in Wilmington, Delaware, our homes came with streams. The realtor saw them more as "dirty, dangerous ditches" and a real negative part of the property; but not me. Give me a stream over an extra bedroom or bathroom anytime! I knew that it would always solve the problem of "Mom, I'm bored!"

So, you see, I have long held a deep appreciation for this form of waterway. Yesterday the appreciation grew deeper. Near Glenorchy, New Zealand, (population – 100) on the South Island, we took a jet boat up the Dart River and the Rock Burn and the Bean Burn. (Burn is a Scottish word for stream.) The streams and the river have the unusual characteristic of constantly changing beds. They are glacier-fed and the bottoms consist of gravel rock which is in continuous motion. The boat navigator must visually read the changing water depths and direction, which is extremely tricky. In just the past twenty-four hours, the river had dropped three feet. Our boat was especially built to only draw four inches of water. Even this little requirement wasn't sufficient to maneuver at certain spots. Skimming over the water, wildly weaving in and out at fifty miles an hour, four times we unexpectedly made 360-degree turns. The boat would totally glide over the water like a skipping rock.

There were nine of us aboard. I sat in the back left-hand corner, in the "wet seat." With mountains, glaciers, meadows, evergreens, ferns, moss, sheep, ducks, deer, black swans, cattle, blue sky, clouds, rain – all going by at a fast speed, I was glad to have the water from the boat occasionally spray me. If I hadn't had that, I would have had to constantly pinch myself to be sure that I wasn't dreaming this "wonder world." I would have ended up black and blue from the required pinches. Instead, I ended up totally soaked, with a Cheshire cat grin on my face, that was slow to wear off.

"Like streams of living water, my soul thirsts for You." That's what kept playing in my brain. I didn't know if it was scriptural or not, but it was sincerely stated over and over in my mind. Our Twentieth Century fast-paced world is like those experienced rivers and streams, don't you think? Constantly changing – constantly requiring adaptations and flexibility.

Often I feel like I'm being out-maneuvered, that it is the world that is in control and not me. And then I remember Who is in control. I'm just along for the glorious ride. I have the corner back "wet seat." My navigator – the Captain of my ship, who can safely read the changing stream with no difficulty at all, who can walk on it – or calm it – or part it if need be – is in eternal charge.

We might get a little wet and there might be a few 360-degree turns – but what a glorious ride! Hop aboard. It's a thrill a minute. The Captain has already bought our tickets – with His life – so it's free for the asking. All aboard!

P.S. When I got home, I found in **John 7:37b-38**, "Jesus stood and cried out saying, 'If any man is thirsty, let him come to Me and drink.' He who believes in Me, as the Scripture said, 'From his innermost being shall flow rivers of living water'."

That boat ride left me with a powerful thirst. Are you a little dehydrated, too? Lord, fill us with Your "living water!"

Your sister in Christ,

Lucy

Precious Group,

"Reach out, reach out and touch someone," as the telephone jingle goes. But what if you can't see to reach out or worse yet, what if you are so inwardly turned, to the point of implosion, that you can't reach out?

I guess the reason this came to mind was that one of the most interesting people on our trip was a lady who was partially blind. I'd never before spent a week on a bus with a blind person. Her husband was our "red team" captain, so that the original thirty was narrowed down to fifteen. There were the "reds" and the "blues." We couldn't possibly have been called the A's and B's or one's and two's, because everyone was an A-type, or at least half of each couple was.

Anyway, there was competition – competition on the big things and competition on the little things. Some bungee jumped, rope swung, microphone sang, danced, water skied, skeet shot, fished, boated, helicoptered, sheep sheared, lined up, boarded and deboarded – Fast – for points. (The red team won.)

Others of us straggled behind and gathered rocks or scenery. Often my partner in "crime" or uncompetitiveness, was this dear blind lady. At first, I thought it was her eyes that slowed her down, not her disposition. But I was wrong. She said that her husband loved to be "on time" and "manage" her and she usually allowed him, but by nature, she was a straggler, too. Yea – a fellow "tagger on" – another "rope wanderer" – (that's someone who likes to explore, as long as they have a rope tethered to home base).

She told me that as a girl of seventeen, she had borrowed some of her mother's fingernail polish – couldn't open the bottle, so tried to heat it over the stove, where it had exploded. It left her totally blind in one eye and partially blind in the other.

"Oh, how awful!" I exclaimed, really getting into the awfulness of that visual loss, when she went on and told of the benefits of the growth opportunities that her loss had afforded. She'd graduated from high school and college with the aide of her friends, who did all required

Teach me to fly.

Mary Barwick

reading for her. She'd married, raised a family, then decided, after years of volunteer work, to go back to school. She earned a degree in counseling and now had her own practice, specializing in marriage counseling.

"Oh, how wonderful!" In five minutes, my "awful" empathy had been transformed into "wonderful elation" – a real metamorphosis. I realized that "reach out, reach out and touch someone" had nothing to do with one's eyesight.

The word "metamorphosis" reminds me of the moth I saw two nights ago, at the lake. Because of traveling, we hadn't been there in almost a month. In that short amount of time, the winter had given way to spring. It was pouring down rain. I felt like the blind man that Jesus laid hands on, twice, in order for the man to see clearly. With Christ's first touch, everything wasn't totally clear, was blurred – like the pouring-down rain distorted this spring beauty. I could see azaleas, dogwoods, fields of blue and white wisteria, and little spring green leaves popping out. Thank goodness, it was storming. It would have been too much to take in – too beautiful to fathom!

I needed gradual exposure – a little blurryness. The raindrops softened the glory, so that it was palatable to my senses. The real thing would have been too much to comprehend. Maybe the blind man also needed a little time to adjust to the glory. It says, "And they brought a blind man to Him and entreated Him to touch him. And taking the blind man by the hand, he brought him out of the village; and after spitting on his eyes, and laying His hands upon him, He asked him, 'Do you see anything?' And he looked up and said, 'I see men, for I am seeing them like trees, walking about.' Then again He laid His hands upon his eyes and he looked intently and was restored and began to see everything clearly." **Mark 8:22-25.** I believe that it was Christ's compassion, not ability, that slowed the healing process down. And I thanked Him for this rain blur that slowed this spring down for me.

Back to the moth. I'm sorry how my brain's bouncing, it must be the jet lag again. Anyway, the first night at the lake the storm grew worse, never letting up. The wind howled – lightning – thunder – I mean, a real "Noah storm." I looked up from writing and there, on the window, was a huge green moth. I said, "Look, Winton, a green butterfly!" He said, "No way!" He rushed outside into the stormy night, to check it out. "It's only a moth," he said. I thought to myself, only a moth? Who said that a moth isn't as big a deal as a butterfly? I mean, it's raining and storming and Noah wouldn't want to go boating tonight and here, flying in for a rest, comes this big beautiful green moth. Let's have a little respect! I mean, I don't see anyone else flying – do you? "Flying in adversity." That's what that moth was doing, "Flying in Adversity."

Now I want to think about "Implosion." I want to consider those who can't "fly in adversity" in the storms of life – those who are so inwardly, self-absorbed or so totally life-crippled, that they not only can't fly, they can't even take off. And the worse scenario is those that implode and disintegrate because of their limited vision. I think of Peter and Judas – both denied and betrayed their Lord. When confronted, one wept bitterly then got up and became a "rock." The other hanged himself. One accepted forgiveness – the other couldn't. One flew – the other crashed and burned.

Much as we'd like to deny it, I think we all have a little Peter and Judas in us. We all are sinners – denyers – even betrayers – at one time or another. The difference is, as Christians – we are to be flyers – getting ready for those eternal wings to come. And what are we to do for those who just can't seem to lift off – for those whose life seems to be stalled or their wings clipped? I suggest, "Reach out, reach out and touch someone," might be just the right approach for a rise to occur.

Isaiah says in **40:31**, "But they that wait upon the Lord shall renew their strength; they shall mount up with wings as eagles; they shall run, and not be weary; and they shall walk and not faint."

Lord, may we take flight, even in adversity. May we carry friends piggyback, if need be, until they get their wings? Oh, but of course, I forgot – You piggybacked us all – through Your Son.

Let's go flying – "up, up and away." You, Lord God – are the "Wind Beneath our Wings."

> Your sister in Christ,
>
> Lucy

Precious Group,

"You can't dream when you're in a fire."

I talked to my beautiful sister, Mary, on the telephone today. She's blonde, blue-eyed and beautiful. Seven years older than I, she's the wise one – the mature one – but also the innocent one, in that there is a freshness about her and a rightness about her that is enchanting.

She was rightly named, for she's the most "motherly" mother, I know. She truly means it when she says, "I love staying at home with my family." She is good at saving things and cleaning closets and actually enjoys folding freshly laundered clothes.

Growing up, my two blonde, blue-eyed older siblings used to unmercifully tease me. One of their favorite taunts was to tell me that it was a secret, but that I was adopted, that's why I had brown eyes and brown hair. (They and I obviously never considered Daddy's contribution, or maybe I didn't know of such things at that point in my development.) Anyway, I would be devastated and run crying to Mama. In fact, I think I probably was a good "wolf-crier" and "tattle-taler."

Thank the dear Lord, they weren't too familiar with the Old Testament story about "color-coated Joseph" and how his siblings got rid of him. A desert ditch might have also become my playground! But instead, only doors were slammed and locked by my sister and I just lost wrestling bouts with my brother. I was better off than Joseph, though I didn't know it at the time! Today, I know they could have both been more convincing in their adoption scam if their argument had been based on closet cleaning instead of hair and eye color. For Mary and I are alike in some ways — but in numerous other ways, there're obviously no shared genes — and that's one of the joys — our differences. I think Mary favors our maternal grandmother, for whom she is named — Mary Adelaide Graves White. Our "Gran," just as the name implies, was "grand!" She was a lady of genteel breeding — a Virginian through and through, and she'd never let you forget it. But more importantly, she was a lady of the highest standards. She knew about one's duty — one's family loyalty. She was dependable and reliable. Her world was disciplined and orderly. Mary follows in those vast footprints and it's fun for me to skip or run or fall behind them. Mary's good with the "sick;" I'm good with the "silly." Mary's good with setting a beautiful table; I'm good with glitter and glue. She brings a warm glow; I bring, perhaps, candy sprinkles.

The point being, we're different and I love the difference. Once a year, Mama gives us a family trip. To spend the night with your sister for a whole week, is wonderful! We have grand "pillow talks." I talk about how blonde and blue-eyed and beautiful she is and she says, "Oh, Lucy! Don't be ridiculous!" — but I know she likes it. And she also sings my praises and I say, "Oh, Mary! Don't be ridiculous!" — But she knows I like it, too! It's fun and reaffirming.

Now we have our own individual families, but our firm foundation gives us a lot of common ground on which to stand. We have four children and so does she. We've shared pictures and problems and boasts and advice.

Today we shared heartaches, which I think, are a lot more painful than headaches. Headaches are more prevalent with diapers and carpools. Aspirin and a solitary bubblebath usually alleviate the symptoms. Heartaches are different. The headaches occur usually while the children are at home, but heartaches are more prevalent when they're gone. The headache communication consists usually of petty bickering — the heartache communication consists usually of long pauses over the telephone. With headache problems – the parents have to initiate the solution. With heartache problems – it's the children's responsibility.

Today, we shared "heartache." I said, "Mary, it's hard to dream when you're in the fire." She asked, "Lucy, is that something that you just thought up or is it a famous quote?" I said, "I don't know, it just popped into my brain, but it is a reality, don't you think?"

I must call her back, for there's more to that reality. I want to add something to that statement. "You can't dream in a fire – but you can sing!" What? It's true! I've read over and over in David's psalms – read time and time again in the psalmist's psalms songs which dealt with heartaches, – hot, hard, horrible times in their lives and those writings were to be sung. They were to be the Hymnal of the Israelites.

And then I think of Shadrach, Meshach and Abednego. And what does tradition have them doing while in the fiery furnace? Sing!

And lastly, I think about "Choir Day" at the "True Divine Baptist Church" this year. I'm an honorary member of this church's choir. One of the biggest thrills in my life is that each year I get to participate in "Choir Day." There were over sixteen choirs from various churches participating, each singing two or three glorious gospel selections. This year, my church choir was honored with an invitation. The service lasted over four hours – most choirs sang and left – but I stayed and I'm so glad I did!

One of the tall pillars of the church whom I'd gotten to know over the past four years had grown even taller – for this year, he was seated in a wheel chair. He had had an accident at work. After all the choirs had sung, he wheeled himself up to the front, and with gracious tears, he thanked his church for their love and their support. Then he started singing – all alone – praising the Lord. It was powerful!

I believe you possibly can't dream in a fire – but you can powerfully sing! And I know of no better way to cool the temperature down and make the fire bearable than with "God-centered" singing. It floats up prayers, I think, right to our almighty Father – Who can renew visions – renew hopes – and renew dreams.

I've got to go call my blonde, blue-eyed, beautiful sister and tell her there's more to the quote.

Your brown-eyed, adopted sister in Christ,

Lucy

Shadrach, Meshach, and Abednego's "Fiery Furnace Song"*

1 O all ye works of the Lord, bless ye the Lord; praise him and magnify him forever.

2 O ye angels of the Lord, bless ye the Lord; praise him and magnify him forever.

3 O ye Heavens; bless ye the Lord; O ye waters that be above the firmament, bless ye the Lord;

4 O all ye powers of the Lord, bless ye the Lord; praise him and magnify him forever.

5 O ye sun and moon, bless ye the Lord; O ye stars of heaven, bless ye the Lord;

6 O ye showers and dew, bless ye the Lord; praise him and magnify him forever.

7 O ye winds of God, bless ye the Lord; O ye fire and heat, bless ye the Lord;

8 O ye winter and summer, bless ye the Lord; Praise him and magnify him forever.

9 O ye dew and frosts, bless ye the Lord; O ye frost and cold, bless ye the Lord;

10 O ye ice and snow, bless ye the Lord; praise him and magnify him forever.

11 O ye nights and darkness, bless ye the Lord; O ye light and darkness, bless ye the Lord:

12 O ye lightning and clouds, bless ye the Lord; praise him and magnify him forever.

13 O let the earth bless the Lord; O ye mountains and hills, bless ye the Lord;

14 O all ye green things upon the earth, bless ye the Lord; praise him and magnify him forever.

15 O ye wells, bless ye the Lord; praise him and magnify him forever.

16 O ye whales and all that move in the waters, bless ye the Lord;

17 O all ye fowls of the air, bless ye the Lord; O all ye beasts and cattle, bless ye the Lord;

18 O ye children of men, bless ye the Lord; praise him and magnify him forever.

19 O ye people of God, bless ye the Lord; O ye priests of the Lord, bless ye the Lord;

20 O ye servants of the Lord, bless ye the Lord; praise him and magnify him forever.

21 O ye spirits and souls of the righteous, bless ye the Lord; O ye holy and humble men of heart, bless ye the Lord;

22 Let us bless the Father, the Son and the Holy Spirit; praise him and magnify him forever.

* A song of creation
Benedicite, Omnia Opera Domini
The Hymnal 1982 according to the use of The Episcopal Church
(based on "The Song of the Three Young Men" in the Apocrypha of the Bible)

Precious Group,

Saturday I went into the woods to pray. Oh, and I am so glad that I did! I had forgotten the awesome holiness found in such a woodland sanctuary. There is a profound quiet – a stillness like no other place. The little noises become more audible – the little movements become more alive. The work of a solitary ant seems to take on more purpose and meaning. The wind blows one single leaf – but not its neighbor, and then, in the next instant, it's the neighboring leaf's turn for a twirl. And pine straw, brown old pine straw, takes on a whole new identity in the woods. It becomes dainty warm icicles, draping branches and rows of little pine straw tents for creature dwellings. Grand!

How did I find myself in such a marvelous spot? Easy — by being the perfect hostess! You see, we had a fantastic Women's Retreat at our lake home. The theme for the day was prayer. We were mightily instructed on how to become stronger "Prayer Warriors." One of our training maneuvers was a 45-minute "alone time" with our Lord. In silence, we dispersed and found solitary sanctuaries. As a hostess, I chose the less popular woods for my retreat and left the choice lake views for the guests. Thank the dear Lord that I did! The woods were a blessing!

I went rushing into the woods because I couldn't wait to get started. And as I walked, my pace slowed — my senses awakened. I had forgotten the joy — the magical joy — of woods. Smells found nowhere else. Sounds of dried leaves crackling underfoot. I did "whish" kicks, just to see and hear them fly. This was a world that I had known, that I had enjoyed, but had failed to revisit for such a long time. Memories flowed — wonderful childhood "make-believe" memories — of neighborhood children creating their own imaginary worlds for a day. I had a grand time mentally walking back in time to this wonderful, whimsical world. But as I walked deeper into the forest, I went deeper into my memories. These magical, make-believe worlds gave way to the mystical reality experienced by a twelve-year-old girl.

Oh — and I remembered — I remembered — my first Solitary Sanctuary — my first Holy Ground created by my one-on-ONE encounter with my heavenly Father. I was attending Camp Desoto in Mentone, Alabama. Each morning we had group prayer, seated around a beautiful lake, and each evening we had group prayer in our cabins, right before "Lights Out." But if you needed or wanted to be alone to pray, you headed for the woods.

One day, I remember being greatly distressed and thus I retreated to this unknown solitary sanctuary. I walked down a windy, woodland path until I came upon a small clearing. There, a huge "tree cross" had been erected. I remember being profoundly moved, thinking this cross was probably much like the original.

And there, for the first time, I met my Lord, one-on-ONE. Of course, there had been numerous times of prayer, previously, but somehow, this was different. I had a problem and there was no Mama or Daddy or friend to turn to for advice or backup prayer. It was a total dependency on God alone. It was just us two against the world. And it was humbling, but all right. I poured out my heart and it was all right. I cried unto Him and it was all right.

What amazed me so much in the reflection was that I couldn't remember the original trauma that had driven me to the woods in the first place. I thought — "Lucy, Alzheimer's!" then I thought — "No, Lucy, your 'mind blank' was Τελοσ-erased."

"Τελοσ-erased" — what in the world is that? Well, let me tell you. It is a grand and glorious thing! Laura Barr told us of a Jewish custom prevalent during Christ's life. Over each prison door "Τελοσ" was stamped when a prisoner had completed his sentence, he paid the price required. Τελοσ meant "It is finished." The same exact words our Lord Jesus said on the cross – "It is finished." He paid the price. Satan was eternally defeated. The communication gaps between God and man no longer existed. The veil had been eternally ripped.

I believe it was because of this act – this "Christ Crucified Act" – that I had my "mind blank." It had been Τελοσ-erased – Christ cleaned!

I couldn't wait to go back to our priest, Father Russell, and share this beautiful image. I did and he took it and expanded the vision – exploded it's horizons into the infinite, where it needed to reign. You see, Father Russell is fluent in Greek. I asked if he would mind looking up **John 19:30** in Greek, to be sure the translation was the same. I wanted to be sure that "Τελοσ" was the exact word used by Christ. Father Russell read, and then smiled. (He smiles a lot.) The exact word Christ used wasn't "Τελοσ" but "Τετελεδται." My blank "Oh," response warranted a fuller explanation. He said that our Lord used the word Τετελεδται, which was a more active version of Τελοσ. He went on to explain that Τελοσ was more like a noun and more passive. It's like "the end," whereas Christ's words for all eternity are more active. A better translation would be "It has been accomplished." The image of a man's debt being paid and having it recorded with a little wooden plaque nailed above his cell comes to mind, versus the image of "The Man" paying off our sins being recorded with His sinless body being nailed to a cross. There is no comparison. One is finite and the other is infinite.

I think I had often settled for the passive Τελοσ version. I had made the empty cell, Christ's tomb – too little – too small – too insignificant, in order that I could have control over the scene. In my version, I could remove the Τελοσ sign and rehash and replay my old sins as I so chose – over and over again. "Lord, please forgive" – one more time – "Lord, please forgive" – one more time. Today, I realized what a disservice I do to my Lord by wanting to rehash old sins – old confessed sins – old forgiven sins – Τελοσ sins. I believe I must have enjoyed replaying the dirt. I believe I must have enjoyed eating and re-eating humble pie. But this is not what we are called to do. If I wanted a humble heart, it should come from looking at the cross – not looking at my old sins. "Lucy, you want humility, then get on your knees and look at your Lord, as he stamps "Τετελεδται" over my confessed sins. Τετελεδται – "It has been accomplished." It has been accomplished! In other words, "Leave it, Lucy – eternally – get on with it – eternally."

I believe we are to live in this Τετελεδται reality. We are to confess our sins, humbly, to our Almighty God. His Son, our Lord Jesus, then as our eternal Intercessor and Most High Priest, takes them to the Father, where we receive the stamp of Τελοσ – the stamp of approval – "It is finished." We are to claim this reality of forgiveness!

I believe there is a glorious dance choreographed by our Lord for each one of us. Millions of *pas de deux* – me and the Lord – you and the Lord. Occasionally, I'm afraid, I've been guilty of trying to take the lead and then He and I get stuck doing the "Box Step," covering the same ground, over and over again. But when I allow Him to take the lead, ah, there is a flow, a grace, as we twirl towards eternity. Then there are no "stuck steps," only leaps of joy!

Τελοσ = Τετελεδται

The end = "It has been accomplished!"

Leap children! Leap for joy!

Your sister in Christ,

Lucy

Precious Group,

If you don't mind, I'd like to mentally go back into the woods. It's been almost a week since that memorable event. And it was just that, a "memorable event," one which I have been mentally savoring and relishing these past days. There's more to be explored in this woodland scene. This "Holy Ground" needs to be mentally revisited once more. For just as Father Russell took Τελοσ = "the end" and expanded my vision to Τετελεδται = "It has been accomplished," I feel my "Holy Ground" understanding needs to be broadened.

What is "Holy Ground?" For me, it's where I meet God "one-on-ONE." It's funny, but the first thing that I was dying to do when I came out of the woods, was to find a rock to place on the very spot where I prayed – to mark the spot. I yearned to say, with a monument or a marker of some sort, that this now was "Holy Ground." I wanted it to be set apart – a God-encountered spot.

Earlier that morning, I had the same strong urge to mark a prayer spot. I wanted my group to sign the wall up in the chaplet of the lake house. (Winton, we didn't.) These six precious ladies are my prayer partners. We have been meeting weekly for over five years – praying, sharing and holding each other accountable in our individual Christian walks. I love them. I wanted them to sign the wall, just a little graffiti to commemorate our first chaplet service. Ever since we had moved into our lake house I wanted – I needed – these precious ladies to come worship our Lord on these premises. Somehow, it would finalize and complete the house. And it did! We held a Morning Prayer service and I wanted signed walls so that for as long as the house stood, this event would be remembered. "Holy Ground," set-apart ground. I understood why mankind, throughout the ages has created Stonehenges and mounds and altars and monuments and churches and cathedrals. They needed and wanted to shout throughout the ages that something extraordinary had happened there: "one-on-ONE" communication occurred. God and man communed.

One of my favorite activities on trips is to seek out the "Holy Grounds." Of course, I love to visit and worship at the various churches and cathedrals, for they are grand and glorious. But the places that I would like to write about and give tours of are unexpected ones, the surprise, serendipity ones: a neon cross from a dorm window, a tree cross in the woods, a one-pew chapel in a huge cathedral, a blue-windowed chapel in a hospital, an airport chapel in New Zealand. You turn a corner and surprise! There's "Holy Ground." It's this unexpected pleasure, this unexpected shout of "Holy Ground Here" that always stops me dead in my tracks. Hold it, busy world, God's here!

But my vision needed to be expanded. At the ladies' lake retreat, you would have loved seeing all the Christian adornments. I have never seen more crosses and fishes and butterflies and doves gathered. We were all marked as Christ's own, not only by the glow of our faces, but by the wonderful Christian jewelry. It became almost a game, recognizing our markings. One person even went so far as interpreting the insignia on my jeans back pocket as two fish kissing.

It's fun to not only come across surprise "Holy Ground" places, but the jewels reminded me of how much fun it is to bump into strangers, walk by strangers, sit by strangers, talk to strangers and notice little gold crosses glittering around their necks. Their strangeness instantly dissolves into recognition of a fellow sister or brother in Christ. My understanding of "Holy Ground" expands to not only include places, but also fellow Christians. If I had to diagram this expanse, I'd say the "one-on-ONE" encounter had been broadened to "one-on-ONE-on-one."

But again, my vision needed to be expanded. And it was, by Mother Teresa. A dear friend lent me the video on this living saint. This week I watched it once, then twice, then a third time. An expansion took place. The diagram of this new "Holy Ground" stretch would be lengthy — in fact, limitless instead of limited. It might look like:

<—one-on-ONE-on-one—>

Some of her love stretches are:

<–Stretch–> "Each individual person has been created to love and to be loved. Hindu, Muslim, Jews, Communists, Christians – doesn't matter. Rest doesn't matter. Religion doesn't matter. Every single man, woman, child, is a child of God, created in the image of God and that's what we look at."

<–Stretch–> "God's love is infinite, full of tenderness, full of compassion. God loves to work through us – you and me. The way you touch people, the way you give to people, that love for one another. It is His love in action through us."

<–Stretch–> "Very often other people mistake the work with the vocation. The work is not the vocation. The vocation is to belong to Jesus."

<–Stretch–> "We need lots of love to forgive, but we need much more humility to ask for forgiveness. I want you to share the joy of loving."

<–Stretch–> "His love in action for us was the crucifixion."

<–Stretch–> "Small things with great love. It is not how much we do, but how much love we put in the doing," and "It's not how much we give, it's how much love we put in the giving."

<–Stretch–> "To God there is nothing small. The moment we have given it to God, it becomes infinite."

<–one-on-ONE-on-one–>

Winton, you can relax. I don't think graffiti is necessary for chaplet-marking. And woods, I believe two knee prints on the ground will suffice for a monument.

"How lovely are Thy dwelling places, O Lord of hosts." Holy Ground Surrounds Us All.

Your sister in Christ,

Lucy

Precious Group,

Guess where I want to go? Do I hear, "Oh, no, not back to the woods?" Sorry. Maybe this will complete the "Woodland Trilogy." All I know is that there is more to the story and it's about prayer. Oh, and it is so very hard for me to write to you about this Holy Communication. It's so very, very personal. I believe each one of us is called to pray – called to commune with our Lord God, in all three forms of His Personage – to the Father, to the Son, and to the Holy Spirit. This "one-on-ONE" communication, I believe is to be the most important activity of our lives. Again, I repeat – it is the most important activity of our lives.

I don't understand the dynamics involved, but I do acknowledge the demand of my Lord God for my attention. My precious friend, Judy Jolly, explained this relationship so simply and beautifully last week. During Holy Communion at our Prayer Retreat, we, the participants, were asked to give the sermon. There was no awkwardness, no "You do it, Mikey" mentality. Humbly, for about thirty minutes, different ladies stood and reverently, but boldly, shared prayer insights. Oh, and I wished that I had a tape recorder, just like I wished that I had a rock to mark my prayer ground. I would have loved to have been able to play and replay those humbly bold declarations of faith. The uniqueness of each testimony reconfirmed the uniqueness of each person's relationship with her God.

Back to Judy, this precious fifty-year-old four-foot-eleven-inch child of God stood and shined. She said, "You know who's voice I love hearing more than any other person's in the world?" We all inwardly nodded. We all knew. You see, Judy loves Robert. Robert is her son, her only son, her only living child, and Judy loves Robert, not in a possessive, smothering way, but in a thanksgiving way. She knows that he is a gift from God. We all know that. With that knowledge, there's no possible room for haughty pride, just humble pride. A constant "Thank you, Lord" exudes with every statement of love about Robert.

Over the years, we friends have watched and enjoyed and relished this child's development into a fine young Christian man. The mama beamed, we beamed, too. Judy loves Robert. She went on to say that she loved hearing Robert's voice in all situations and under all circumstances. We all inwardly agreed. She then went on to proclaim that if she, the sinner, thirsted for this communication with her child, think how much our God, the Sinless Creator, thirsted for His children's communications. "Yes!" I repeat, "Yes! Amen, sister!" I inwardly proclaimed.

You mean my prayer doesn't need to be perfect? That I don't need to clean up my act before the "Prodigal Daughter" returns to her Father? You mean He wants to hear from me, just as I am, now? With the words and heart and mind that I have today? Wow!

Again, I think of a mother and her child and their communication skills. Over and over, I've seen a mother interpret her baby's – then toddler's – then teen's – then adult child's words. "Ga Ga" is what I hear the infant say, but his interpreter, his mother, beams and translates the utterance to "I would like some more juice with my cereal, please, Mother dear and I love you."

Oh, how a mother and child can commune and that is what we are to do – commune "one-on-ONE" with our Father – commune – daily – commune – just as we are – commune.

We often end our prayers with "Through Jesus Christ our Lord." I believe He is our translator. He takes our baby-talk and stands in the presence of His Father, and because of His Crucifixion, can translate our broken utterances into acceptable prayers.

Again, I want to repeat, I don't understand all the dynamics, but I do feel the call – the call to commune with the Almighty. It's like a magnet, a pull towards my Creator. I can ignore the pull, can fill my world with busyness, but the pull is always there. It is a constant and the constant does call me.

Again, I don't know how it works, but I feel somehow that it is very much like Lake Martin's Dam. There was a flood two weeks ago and the power company had to open twelve of the flood gates. We went to observe this rare power phenomenon. A huge crane traveled along the dam and hoisted the massive gates, allowing the water to flow. (How much water, Winton? "Three million gallons per gate per minute = thirty-six million gallons per minute for twelve gates – two billion, one-hundred-sixty million gallons per hour – fifty-one billion, eight-hundred-forty million gallons per day) "Oh." A lot of water was passing through the dam.

I believe an analogy can be made. I believe that Christ takes our prayers, just as they are. I believe that He is like the gate operator. He empowers our prayers, makes them acceptable to our Father and as a result, the gates are lifted, God's grace flows. I believe our prayers – through Christ – empower God's grace to flow. That is an awesome statement. Almost too profound to utter – but I believe it – I confess it. Our "one-on-ONE" communication is empowered by the Crucified Christ.

I'm sitting out on a wonderful deck at a lodge. When I started writing to you, it was before 6:00 a.m. and dark. I pulled a chair up under a lamp post to see. As the day broke, the light automatically went off. I looked up and much to my delight, found that I was seated under a beautiful dogwood tree and that the lamp post that had illumined my darkness was cross shaped, having a lamp attached to each of its arms.

"Lord, let your light shine on me," was my prayer song. And that was enough, I think, acceptable, I think, for it was a spill-over from my heart. I've read books on prayer. I've practiced different techniques of prayer. I've named them, categorized them, planned them – but still, I believe the ones that are most acceptable – most pleasing to my Lord – are heart-spills – love overflows. Sometimes joyful. Sometimes desperate cries. Sometimes baby-talk. But we have the Translator to help with the communication – "one-on-ONE."

I don't like to drive in the dark, for I can't see very well. But when necessary, if driving from the lake, I make a point of taking the route that goes by this small insignificant-looking red brick church. You wouldn't notice it during the day, but at night it takes on a "Holy Ground" glow. For one whole wall at the side of the front door is lighted. It's a huge stained-glass picture of our Lord Jesus praying in Gethsemane. You only notice it in the dark, for it's only illumined then – but at night it shines.

It powerfully reminds me of Christ praying and we are called to be "imitators of Christ." That's enough of a command to pray, don't you think?

"And it came about while He was praying in a certain place, after He had finished, one of His disciples said to Him, 'Lord teach us to pray,' and He said to them, 'When you pray, say:'" [1]

Our Father who art in heaven,

Hallowed be Thy name.

Thy kingdom come.

Thy will be done,

On earth as it is in heaven

Give us this day our daily bread.

And forgive us our debts, as we forgive our debtors.

And lead us not into temptation,

but deliver us from evil.

For thine is the kingdom, and the power, and the glory, forever.

Amen[2]

Your sister in Christ,

Lucy

[1]Luke 11:1
[2]Matthew 6:9-13

T'was the Week Before Easter

T'was the week before Easter,
And all through the house,
I made piles of your letters,
Instead of meals for my spouse.

There were forty-two of them,
Only ten more to go.
They were stacked on the pool table,
In a neat little row.

Each packed in a folder,
All yellow and bright,
Which had been glued and decorated.
Oh, what a bright sight!

I was waiting – anticipating –
Letter 43
Which would be about Easter
I was sure as could be!

Quietly giving God pep talks,
The idea of such!
"Lord, you know this one's important,
So I'm expecting pretty much."

"Lucy Blount, on your knees,
I think you should get!
This isn't your project.
If it is, — I quit."

Thank goodness, the Lord
Got me back on the track –
Of who's Boss and the Leader
And I better sit back.

You see, Mary Barwick
Called on the phone.
She declared herself crazy.
"Would I visit her in a 'Home'?"

"Mary, my dear,
Please tell me what's wrong?
If you go to the hospital,
Then I'll come along."

"For you know, this isn't
Just your little dream.

For we're in this together,
What a fabulous team!"

"Well Lucy,
Please tell me,
Have you written a letter
That deals with flying in very bad weather?"

"Why Mary, of course!
How did you know?
It's letter 38.
Who told you so?"

She said, "I was painting,
And out of the blue,
Came 'Teach me to fly,'"
And she just knew.

"Oh!" I exclaimed –
With a lump in my throat.
Then there was silence – more silence –
More silence – no "gloat."

I ran up the stairs,
Ripped open her file,
Read the letter to her
And there was no denial.

"Mary," I apologized,
"I was to bring you the next twelve,
But I was waiting for Easter
So I could be a 'bunny elf.'"

"I'll stop what I'm doing –
Put everything on halt.
I should have brought you the letters –
It's really my fault."

The good news, people,
Is even if I blow it,
Mary can keep painting a letter
Even if I don't show it!

For you see, on this project,
We're not in control.
If we try to be bosses,
Then it will be indefinitely put on "hold."

Precious Group,

"Expect a miracle!" one of the TV evangelists used to proclaim, and it would make me a little nervous. I mean, how would I be able to fit a "miracle" into my busy schedule? Why, it just wouldn't look right penciled in my daily planner – April 5th, 2:05 – "miracle." I'd have to hide it at meetings or at least smudge the word, so that I would be the only one "to whom it may concern." For you see, "miracles" in this mechanized, computerized, compartmentalized world, make people very nervous. All of our lives, the world preaches control, control, control. Divide and conquer. But how does one control or divide a miracle? In the *Merriam-Webster Dictionary*, a miracle is defined as "an extraordinary event manifesting a supernatural world of God." Ah Ha!

Yes, "Ah Ha!" The occurrence recorded in "T'was the Week Before Easter" did actually occur. Yesterday, as a matter of fact. And you can testify to the fact that I am no Emily Dickinson. In fact, Winton's critique was, "a little forced iambic pentameter, don't you think?" And I responded with, "Yes dear, how perceptive of you." But the good news is, and I don't know why, but if you add a little Dr. Seuss-type rhyme and humor to hard-to-swallow reality, it seems to go down much easier, especially if you are talking about miracles or "Ah Ha's."

You see, yesterday, right when Winton walked in the door, I bombarded him with the "letter happenings." I was thrilled to see him. I had wanted to share this amazing occurrence with my best friend. I wanted his reaction to be identical to mine – for him to totally share in my amazement and wonder. So I talked fast, fast, fast, but from the very start, I sensed that I was losing him. I could sense a lack of communication, so I talked even faster, as he mentally slipped away. Oh, what a disappointment! I couldn't recapture or transfer the "awe of the afternoon." This precious man could perceive my disappointment. (It wasn't hard, for I was almost in tears.) He even went as far as to say, "I'm sorry. I don't see it the same way you do, and what do these ducks in the painting have to do with flying?" With regained composure, I calmly stated, "The angel is teaching the baby ducks how to fly." "Oh." Again, a courtesy statement, not a comprehending one. "Bye, I love you – see you in Atlanta tomorrow." Did I note a relieved rushing to the door, an escape exit taken? Late last night, we talked on the phone and verbalized our different perspectives. Winton said that he didn't see the "afternoon occurrence" as a miracle. I said, "What about a 'neat happening' and an 'ah ha!'?" And he said, "Yes." He agreed that it was an "Ah ha!" Yes! Communication reigned once more.

Forget the labeling of the event. "You say tomato and I say to-mah-to. You say potato and I say po-tah-to." If asked, I would define "Ah ha!" as an extraordinary event manifesting a supernatural work of God, similar to a miracle, but more "user friendly" to 20th century man.

Miracles, or even "Ah Ha's," how does one comprehend the incomprehensible? How does one translate the non-translatable? How does one transfer the non-transferable? How does one re-create the God created?

I think of the Jewish people of today. I believe that their identity is strong because they have taken an event which occurred over four thousand years ago, to a small group of desert nomads, and have been able to revitalize that desert walk in such a way that it has become a personal journey reality, relived generation after generation. A total faith walk — a total "chosen people" mentality has been ingrained into the very fiber of their being, empowering them to withstand unbelievable anti-Semitism throughout their history, because they believe to the core of their being that they have a uniquely special relationship with their God.

And for us — as Christians — do we have that same bedrock — miracle mentality? Is our Apostles' Creed proclamation, which is proclaimed daily throughout most of our "anno Domini" years — a truly present, faith-walk proclamation? "Anno Domini" — in the year of our Lord — a present, relevant reality?

The Apostles Creed

I believe in God,
the Father Almighty,
creator of heaven and earth.
I believe in Jesus Christ, his only Son, our Lord.
He was conceived by the power of the Holy Spirit
and born of the Virgin Mary.
He suffered under Pontius Pilate,
was crucified, died, and was buried.
He descended to the dead.
On the third day he rose again.
He ascended into heaven,
and is seated at the right hand of the Father.
He will come again
to judge the living and the dead.
I believe in the Holy Spirit,
the holy Catholic Church,
the communion of saints,
the forgiveness of sins,
the resurrection of the body,
and the life everlasting.

Amen

The Book of Alternative Services of the Anglican Church of Canada

Miracles are Mighty Moments. They are God-filled happenings. And "Hear Ye, Hear Ye " to all users of daily planners: There needs to be some rescheduling of our time to allow for and include more "ah ha" and "miracle" time, for they are a present reality!

Ladies and Gentlemen: reschedule your daily schedules!

Your sister in Christ,

Lucy

Precious Group,

"It's Sunday, so I must be in Salt Spring Island, British Columbia." My mama had read me our itinerary over the phone the day before. You see, I didn't know where I was going. (Do we really ever?) I knew the general direction and the duration, but as for the details, I was at a loss.

This is not an unusual occurrence in my life. In our twenty years of marriage, we've been extremely fortunate and blessed by going on frequent trips and excursions. I've learned that in order for me to survive these whirl-wind journeys, I must remain flexible. I used to plan, pack, and prepare far in advance. I would have everything and everybody organized and informed.

Then, right in midstream, everything would be changed. I mean everything. I would have to call relatives and friends and baby-sitters back and give them the latest updated bulletin. I would have to repack and reorganize. I would get a headache and say, in an exasperated tone, "Is this worth it? I wish we could stick to the original plans!" This inflexible attitude would usually result in a few more changes thrown in, just for the fun (Winton's fun) of it. "Can't you be more flexible, Lucy?" was the battle cry. He'd then continue, "Well, I'll just find somebody else to go with me." This would always get my attention and a quick surrender resulted.

For, early on, my mother wisely advised me that whenever my husband asked me to travel with him, "Go, or he will stop asking you." I mean, drop everything. A regimented weekend with my four children, alone, or a loose, flexible one with my husband. Which would you choose? "Go, girl, go!" I did and I do. So that now, after twenty years of conditioning, I can proudly proclaim, "I can be flexible." As a matter of fact, I'm so flexible, that you might call me Loosey Goosey.

I've also learned to sit next to Winton on plane rides, if at all possible. It alleviates the embarrassing "no knowledge" syndrome. I've been asked by nice, unknown seatmates, "Where are you going?" "I don't know." I've been asked, "How long will you be staying?" "I don't know." I've been asked, "How long will you be gone?" "I don't know."

Surely you jest, Lucy? No. In all actuality, this has happened. And you can see the person thinking, "Is this lady real or what? She definitely has a serious problem. She doesn't know whether she's coming or going." Which is often true, and very perceptive of them. But at least my attitude has vastly improved and my headaches are not so frequent, and I'm still invited to "go, girl, go!"

And at this very moment, at 7:00 a.m. Pacific daylight time, I know where I am – Salt Spring Island, British Columbia. (I'm sure because it's on the phone book.) And I do know where I'm going at 9:15 – to St. George's Anglican Church, for it is Palm Sunday and "Triumphal Entries" are being recreated all over the world.

I'm very disappointed that I'm not home. (Lucy, you should be ashamed. This place is beautiful and it will be fine to worship with unknown fellow Christians.) But, I surely would like to have a palm cross from my own church. I surely would like to celebrate Christ's Triumphal Entry into Jerusalem with my known flock. I surely would like getting ready for Holy Week with... "Lucy, hush! Get ready for the King – yourself!"

My Lord comes strongly today. Almost two thousand years ago, He rode a donkey into town. Men, women, and children excitedly rushed into the streets carrying palm branches, waving them freely, and a sea of palms parted as He entered Jerusalem. Just as the Red Sea parted to save the Israelites from Pharaoh's army, the palms parted, marking the route that the King of Kings would take to save us all. Jerusalem, to the cross. He knew the route He was to take. I believe He knew it with His total being. I believe He knew the course He was on. I believe His destination was determined by His free will – to do, totally, His Father's will. Totally.

The palm bearers did not know the course of events that would mark this Holy Week. They were just along for the ride, much like I often am – but what a ride! A 'Ride On, Ride On In Majesty" was taking place right before their very eyes.

The journey continues today, all over the world. Christ's Palm Sunday entry into Jerusalem continues. Christ's Good Friday "Via Dolorosa" walk to the cross continues. Christ's Easter Rise continues. Christ's Ascension continues until His coming again. "Ride On, Ride On In Majesty" – my Lord Jesus, come quickly!

The Sunday of The Passion

The Liturgy of The Palms

Today we greet him as our King, although we know his crown is thorns and his throne a cross. We follow him this week from the glory of the palms to the glory of the resurrection by way of the dark road of suffering and death. United with him in suffering on the cross, may we share his resurrection and new life.
Amen

The Hebrews acclaimed Jesus as Messiah and King,

With palm branches in their hands, crying Hosanna in the highest.

May we also, carrying these emblems, go forth to meet Christ

and follow him in the way that leads to eternal life;

who lives and reigns in glory with you and the Holy Spirit, now and forever.

    Amen

Almighty God,

Whose Son was crucified yet entered into glory,

May we, walking in the way of the cross,

Find it is for us the way of life;

through Jesus Christ our Lord

who is alive and reigns with you

and the Holy Spirit

One God, now and for ever.

    Amen

Excerpts from *The Book of Alternative Services of the Anglican Church of Canada*

The March is on...

Your sister in Christ,

Lucy

The Church of the Ascension

Palm Sunday

Anthem

Ex Ore Innocentium

Bishop W.W. How

It is a thing most wonderful,

Almost too wonderful to be,

That God's own Son should come – from heav'n,

And die... to save a child like me.

And yet I know that it is true:

He chose a poor and humble lot,

And wept, and toiled and mourned, and died,

For love of those who loved him not.

I sometimes think about the Cross,

And shut my eyes, and try... to see

The cruel nails and crown of thorns,

And Jesus crucified for me...

But even could I see him die,

I should but see... a little part...

Of that great love,

which, like a fire,

is always burning in his heart.

And yet I want to love thee, Lord;

O light the flame within my heart,

And I will love thee more and more

Until I see thee

as thou art.

Precious Group,

I have found another job possibility, one which can be performed at my present skill level. I can be a "toilet paper roller folder." A what? A "toilet paper roller folder." In this hotel, much to my delight and surprise, each bathroom is equipped with not one but two toilet paper holders. And if that's not enough folderol fanciness, each end of the tissue is daily folded into a triangle and a pretty sticker placed on it. Yes! I can do this! Another job opportunity!

In this 1990's world, I am a member of an almost extinct breed. I don't have a "work number." And sometimes it bothers me. Every time I write a check, I'm reminded of this shortcoming, for I'm invariably asked to give my "work number." I usually respond with, "I'm sorry, please forgive me, but I don't have one." I feel like I'm met with disbelieving eyes, ones which even question the worth of my check.

"Well, where can you be reached during the day?" "Well, let's see, on Mondays you usually can catch me at Lake Martin, that number ____. (It is blank, not because of secrecy, but because of a blank mind. I can't remember numbers.) "On the way up, I usually stop near St. Margaret's Hospital for a cup of decaffeinated coffee. I usually go through the drive-in, but you could possibly page me and they'd let me talk to you on their phone if we kept our conversation under three minutes. That number is ____. Then, of course, you can reach me at the French's General Store, right outside of Eclectic, Alabama, at about 2:00. I always stop there on the way home to see their new baby and buy a diet coke. Their number is ____. Oh, yes, I almost forgot, I usually say "hi" to Spike and Sharon at Smith's Store, just to be neighborly. Their number is____. Usually I get home by 3:00 and go to the grocery store. That number is ____. (I love this grocery because they give me a check cashing card, so I don't have to weekly go through this "no number" humiliation. For this, I am truly grateful and thus affectionately carry their card next to my favorite credit card.) Then on Tuesday, you can reach me..."

I could go on indefinitely like this and would have to conclude with, "Of course, all numbers are subject to travel changes." At this point, I am sure they'd tear up the check in my face. As you see, I can provide "day-time" numbers, but not a "work number."

My heightened awareness of this shortcoming has made me look for possible job opportunities, not to apply, but just to mentally file away. I give myself a mental pep talk of "you precious child of God, you could be a 'toilet paper roller folder' if you wanted. You are perfectly qualified for this profession. You could have a 'work number' if you wanted."

One thing that I like about this specialized profession is that an ordinary item, with a little bit of attention, takes on a whole new perspective. You actually take notice of the product. Whereas, under normal circumstance, it is only noticed if not available or if it's of poor quality. But, when you take the ordinary, or even the ugly, and give it a little attention, it can become more noticeable and precious.

Two days ago I saw a similar transformation on a much grander scale at the "Butchart Gardens," located right outside Victoria, British Columbia. This fabulous horticultural master-piece was created in the early part of the century by a housewife who didn't like her back yard.

It had previously been a limestone quarry and huge earth gashes resulted. She asked her husband if she could do a little beautification planting. And thus, today we have the glorious "Sunken Garden," the glorious "Japanese Garden," the glorious "Italian Garden." And the *pièce de rèsistance* is the glorious "Rose Garden," built on their tennis court. Can't you imagine the conversation. "Honey, I'm tired of this old game. Why, I even lost today. Would you mind awfully if we planted roses in its place?"

She took something ugly and with love and attention (and a supportive husband) transformed these earth gashes into glorious jewels. It was because of her care and concern that these gaping holes became glorious gardens.

To continue her beautification theme, today they've even gone so far as to plant box gardens on top of every trash receptacle on the property, indoors and out. Wonderful little gardens bloom on top of the garbage. (I wonder what our landscape architect would think of the idea of using planted garbage receptacles in our side yard as opposed to his serpentine bedding design? Just a thought.)

The thought I'm really mulling over, the one that is churning in my mind, is the extraordinary results that occur when a little love and attention is showered on the typically unloved and the typically unattended. Over and over, it was to those people that our Lord Jesus went. Beggars, prostitutes, lepers, tax collectors, blind, lame, deranged... dead. The lonely, the sick, the poor, the broken-hearted. Jesus came. It is to those people, that we might have discounted, that we might have written off, that we might have slammed the door, that we might have stepped over, to whom our Lord came.

He saw no garbage when it came to His fellowman — just God-created brothers and sisters. Fallen, yes, but garbage, no.

And that is what we all need to be totally aware of this Holy Week and each holy week of the year. I'm sure we're very good at being able to list our shortcomings and our sins, on a moment's notice, even alphabetize them if necessary. And I believe it's important that we be able to perform this exercise.

I believe its important to remember the reality of our human frailty and fallenness, keeping our hearts humbly prostrated to our Lord God. But there is a difference in being humble and being humiliated. Our Lord Jesus never humiliated, but met each person at the exact point of their brokenness and allowed them to become whole, with a humble heart – a Christ-filled, humble heart.

It is in humility that we are to greet our brothers and sisters. It is in humility that we are to walk this walk, this Christ-created walk of the cross. The Victory is His. We're just walking in it – following the crowd down the "Via Dolorosa."

He said, "Take up your cross and follow me." This week, can you close your eyes and open your heart and imagine the three men bleeding and beaten, stumbling down this narrow road, heavily laden by the weight of their crosses. And can you imagine the two thieves doubly burdened, not only by their own crosses, but also by their guilt weight? And then there was Jesus – our Lord Jesus – the Innocent – walking in the will of His Father, burdened by our sins. Oh, what a heavy weight. What a humiliation for Him. The crowd – yelling and screaming and spitting and mocking Him. The borne humiliation, in order that we could walk humbly with our God once more.

"Take up your cross and follow me." "Yes Lord!" Do you see the blossoms bursting forth from the old garbage receptacles? – our old garbage receptacles. Can you envision them being transformed into temples, Holy Spirit-filled temples?

Our Lord Jesus Comes

Bloom in His Light

Fair Creatures

God's Creatures

Nothing God Created Should Be Man-Minimized

Pray for me and this book. May it be to His Glory.

Your sister in Christ,

Lucy

Precious Group,

Well, here we are back in Whistler, British Columbia planning a conference. The last time I wrote you from this location was on Christmas Day, while sitting on top of Blackcomb mountain. It was one of the most glorious of Christ's Days that I've ever experienced. For being surrounded by family love, awesome mountains, and not one Christmas tree but tens of thousands, was indescribably delicious. (Not having to cook wasn't bad either!) The whole day was a most fitting and appropriate celebration of our Lord's birth.

Today this world looks different, for the snow has melted and the flowers have blossomed. It's 6:00 in the morning here (9:00 at home), so I've been sitting in the lobby drinking coffee and reading Morning Prayer. I've had my own cathedral window for this worship time, for an entire wall is glass. The mountains and sky and clouds have been awakening before my very eyes with this dawning light. I mean, I've really experienced the ultimate "Green Peace!" These big old ten-thousand-year-old mountains have been silently shouting, "Good morning! Look at us. We're God-made and lady, what's your story?"

My story is similar and so is yours, actually. I mean "God-made." Maybe we're not quite as old or quite as grand, although I've had my moments of feeling both. (Lucy, shame.)

Besides sharing this common heritage of being Creator-made, there also is the ancient obsession of ours to mountain-climb. I don't know why, but I believe that from day one (or was that day six?) when Adam hit the Garden running, he probably started running uphill. When he and his fellow "sons of Adam" (à la C.S. Lewis) were late for dinner, it was because of mountain climbing, not valley dipping, don't you think?

So, ladies and gentlemen, we have mountains to climb. This is part of the universal human experience, just as much as breathing. And how are we to be equipped for these uphill battles, and I do mean battles? We are to piton plant. What? Piton plant.

Let me explain. While driving from Vancouver to Whistler, we occasionally passed sheer mountain rock faces hundreds of feet high. My eyes would focus on little specks clinging to these black granite rocks. I realized that these were not "spidermen," but mountain climbers. I remembered from my teenage experiences in this sport, that even though not visible, these adventurers were not as adventurous and the climb not as perilous as it would seem, for they had pitons. A piton is like a metal cleat. You climb a few feet, then hammer a piton into the mountain, secure a rope which has already been attached to you through the piton and then keep climbing. It acts like a vertical safety net, for in case you fall, it would be a slight descent, not a disaster.

I believe as Christians we have pitons available for our "life climbs." Of course, we have the Holy Trinity as our ultimate Guide, along with the Holy Bible as our Guidebook — and then there's the Communion of Saints and the Universal Church, plus the all-out S.O.S., prayer. I mean, we have numerous piton possibilities so that we can be totally equipped for our journeys.

This reminds me of a precious, precious friend whose family is going through "holy hell" right now. I use that description because from a distance, the situation might look like plain old "hell on earth," but closer up, you realize that there is another Dimension present. The "hell" is a "holy hell" because Christ is right there in it. His pitons are all in place. The safety net is up. The situation has been "fireproofed" by the blood of the Lamb. Of course, there are moments – long moments – of pain and anxiety, like a six-foot mountain drop might cause – but then the rope catches, the pitons hold and "the peace which passeth all understanding" comes back into play.

Frantic friends wonder how can she smile? How can she function normally? That's our question asked from a distance, but then when we get up closer and spend some time with her – we know! Her witness is strong. Christ is in control, not Satan's chaos.

Right now, your climb might seem impossible or you've possibly experienced a sudden six-foot drop. Whatever, remember that you've only experienced a slight descent, not a disaster. Let those Christian "pitons" catch you. Let His everlasting arms hold you. Relax in them. Renew your strength in Him. And then, when you're ready, continue the climb, just be sure to keep piton planting as you go.

The appointed Psalm for today's reading was **Psalm 66**. Verses 7-11 really spoke to me.

7   Bless our God, you people;
       make the voice of this praise to be heard;

8   Who holds our souls in life,
       and will not allow our feet to slip.

9   For you, O God, have proved us;
       you have tried us just as silver is tried.

10   You brought us into the snare;
       you laid heavy burdens upon our backs.

11   You let enemies ride over our heads;
       we went through fire and water;
       but you brought us out into a place of refreshment.

What kind of a snare do you find yourself in today? Maybe it's not a snare, but rather God's safety net. Just a thought. To Him be the glory!

Your sister in Christ,

Lucy

Precious Group,

"Lucy, what are you doing?"

I'm sitting outside, up top. It's late. The moon is shimmering on the water. The air is cool and crisp. It's very quiet – thinking quiet – praying quiet. And that's what I needed – a total still. And this was hard to come by, for inside, on all levels, there are family and friends watching TV or playing games. I just arrived with the groceries and the dog. I've hugged and kissed everyone. I've unpacked and put away. Now I've retreated to the top.

I'm not trying to be anti-social or unfriendly. I'm sure that I'll get into the swing of things in just a little while, but right now – right this very moment, I need to be alone. I need to re-think the happenings of the last few hours.

You see, it's Maundy Thursday and I've been in a garden that I've never experienced before. It was located in our chapel. "In our chapel?" Yes, and that's what I've got to sort through. For me, the Maundy Thursday service has always been one of the most meaningful. In our church, it is held at night. It has always had a very somber, solemn atmosphere, ending with the "stripping of the altar." After we have had our "Last Supper" with the Lord, a reenactment of the first Last Supper, the choir recesses to the back of the church in total silence. You could hear a pin drop or a nail hammered in this quiet. The church is dimmed. A minister reads from Psalms, words that sound as if they could have been ripped from the heart of Christ. Ones that He could have yelled from the cross. And as these soul cries are being made, you see through that darkness, movement at the front of the church. You know what is going on and that makes it even more poignant. Everything is being stripped from the altar – all the hangings, the kneelers, even the cross is taken away. At the same time, you feel like you are being stripped. All your sins of the year are being exposed – all your shortcomings are being exposed. The lights are finally brought back up and all that remains on the alter, totally alone, is a black-draped cross, ready for Good Friday.

But this year was different. And that's what I need to sort through. There was actually a moment of joy in the service. It was like a brief Easter preview. Our processional hymn was actually upbeat. As we practiced it before the service, we choristers were quietly mumbling, "surely this is a mistake." We have an interim minister. We'll just have to humor him, but next year surely we can get back to the old funeral-like dirge. When we processed into the church, the lights were on full brightness, the altar hangings were festival white–bridal white. And during the service, we actually said and sang an "alleluja." To my way of thinking, this was a big "no-no." For in our church's tradition, the 40 days of Lent are a penitent time, a walking-in-the-desert-type experience and all "allelujas" are deleted from the service until Easter, when we burst forth with the angels to sing the "allelujas" to our risen Lord. But not on Maundy Thursday! This is too much! Don't mess with my service – please! (Notice the possessive adjective.) Why, even in each window sat empty copper Easter Lily containers. I'm on the Altar Guild and my puffing up when things aren't just so, I'm afraid, does occur. I kept thinking, surely there's been a mistake. The lily containers look awful empty. Then I realized that the altar would soon look empty and awful, too. It would look like a sacrificial altar, waiting for a body – the Body.

During the sermon, Father Russell explained all of the changes. Thank goodness, for I was about to raise my hand and say that someone had obviously read the church calendar incorrectly, for we've got the wrong service being conducted. This was supposed to be Maundy Thursday service!

He explained that it was indeed Maundy Thursday. That in the older traditions of our church history, on this one day during Lent, for a brief moment, there was a reprieve from the fasting. The "allelujas" and the white hangings represented that "joy burst" – the joy of our Lord's gift to us of His Last Supper, our Holy Communion. Such a gift demanded such a response.

He then showed us an embroidered maniple which hung from his left forearm. He said that it represented the towel which Jesus used when He washed and dried His disciples' feet on this Holy night. That it once was used by all of the clergy as they administered Holy Communion to remind them of their call to servanthood. He instructed us that after the Holy Eucharist, there would be the stripping of the cross. The lights would remain on and that we would read responsively Psalm 22.

I thought, you mean, we are actually going to see what's going on and we're going to actually have to say those awful verses, those "heart-ripping" ones? We're going to have to personally participate in this stripping? Why? I'll feel like I've been "strip-searched." But maybe that's the point. He then said that the unused wine and bread would be placed on the chapel altar, which had been turned into a garden of flowers to remind us of the Garden of Gethsemane.

"What? Flowers? You've got to be kidding?" After the initial shock wore off, I finally sat back and relaxed and enjoyed and even relished the "old" – but – "new" traditions. After the stripping of the altar, Father Russell pulled out a dust cloth and dusted the whole altar.

Again, as an Altar Guild representative, I wanted to run and say, "Really, that's not necessary — we keep everything spotless!" But then I realized that he was just getting it more spotless, so that it could represent holding tomorrow the Spotless One. (When I asked, he said that again was one of the oldest church traditions, not only to wipe, but wash the altar on Maundy Thursday.) "Oh."

We recessed. I changed and then went into the chapel garden to pray. It was beautiful! This beauty came not only from the blossoms and their perfume, but also from the room full of worshippers praying on their knees. We had just finished an hour and a half service and the prayers continued. We were told that the praying would continue all through the night. People had signed up for 30-minute intervals and there would be continuous praying until the first hour on the cross tomorrow.

I wanted to take a shift! I wanted to feel like I was in the Garden of Gethsemane with my Lord this one night — but no. I had the groceries melting in the car. I had to go to the lake.

So alone, in the dark, with only the companionship of our dog, Daisy, I took this 45-minute drive. I couldn't pick up my favorite Christian radio station, so I turned to the classical one. They were playing Tchaikovsky's "Swan Lake." It was perfect for my mood. For my drive felt more like a flight from Gethsemane. "Lucy, where are you going?" "I've got the groceries, Lord. I can't stay and pray in the garden."

I arrived and wanted to write to you, but I was so tired. I did get the first paragraph written, but then retreated to the sofa for just a little rest. My walk down the stairs to our bedroom felt like another Gethsemane retreat. I laid down on the sofa in front of the fire. It felt so comfortable. I had all the good intentions of resting for just a little while, then getting up and finishing your letter. But, no. My last thought before falling asleep was, I bet the disciples went to sleep around a fire in the garden that night so long ago. "Lord, I'm so tired — just like Peter and John. I'm truly sorry. 'The spirit is willing, but the flesh is weak.'" **Matthew 26:41.**

When I awoke, it was in the middle of the night. Winton was sound asleep, but as I crawled into bed, he said, "What are you doing?" I wanted to say, "I was trying to stay up with my Lord, to mentally and spiritually be in His garden tonight. I wanted to stay awake and keep vigil with Him just for this one night, but I fell asleep." But before I could answer, Winton was again soundly sleeping, so I lay down, looked out the window at the moon and stars and darkness. "Lord, tomorrow we commemorate the real darkness, the one only You could pierce. Lord, I wanted so much to stand by Your side tonight, to be firmly planted on my knees with You.

But Lord, I slept, just as Your earlier disciples did. But Lord, I love You, just as they did. It's just that "the spirit is willing, but the flesh is weak." But then, You know.

Goodnight. Until tomorrow –

Lucy

Psalm 22
Psalm of the Cross

1   My God, my God, why hast Thou forsaken me?

    Far from my deliverance are the words of my groaning.

2   O my God, I cry by day, but Thou dost not answer; and by night, but I have no rest.

3   Yet Thou art holy, O Thou who art enthroned upon the praises of Israel.

4   In Thee our fathers trusted; They trusted, and Thou didst deliver them.

5   To Thee they cried out and were delivered; In Thee they trusted, and were not disappointed.

6   But I am a worm, and not a man, a reproach of men, and despised by the people.

7   All who see me sneer at me; They separate with the lip, they wag the head saying,

8   "Commit yourself to the Lord; let Him deliver him; Let Him rescue him, because He delights in him."

9   Yet Thou art He who didst bring me forth from the womb;

    Thou didst make me trust when upon my mother's breasts.

10   Upon Thee I was cast from birth; Thou hast been my God from my mother's womb.

11   Be not far from me, for trouble is near; For there is none to help.

12   Many bulls have surrounded me; Strong bulls of Bashan have encircled me.

13   They open wide their mouth at me, as a ravening and a roaring lion.

14   I am poured out like water, and all my bones are out of joint;

    My heart is like wax; It is melted within me.

15   My strength is dried up like a potsherd, and my tongue cleaves to my jaws;

    and Thou dost lay me in the dust of death.

16   For dogs have surrounded me; a band of wildoers has encompassed me;

    They pierced my hands and my feet.

17   I can count all my bones. They look, they stare at me;

18   They divided my garments among them, and for my clothing they cast lots.

19   But Thou, O Lord, be not far off; O Thou my help, hasten to my assistance.

20   Deliver my soul from the sword, My only life from the power of the dog.

21   Save me from the lion's mouth; and from the horns of the wild oxen. Thou dost answer me.

22   I will tell of Thy name to my brethren; In the midst of the assembly I will praise Thee.

23   You who fear the Lord, praise Him; All you descendants of Jacob,

    glorify Him, and stand in awe of Him, all you descendants of Israel.

24   For He has not despised nor abhorred the affliction of the afflicted;

    Neither has He hidden His face from him; But when he cried to Him for help, He heard.

25   From Thee comes my praise in the great assembly; I shall pay my vows before those who fear Him.

26   The afflicted shall eat and be satisfied; Those who seek Him will praise the Lord.

    Let your heart live forever!

27 All the ends of the earth will remember and turn to the Lord,
      and all the families of the nations will worship before Thee.
28 For the kingdom is the Lord's, and He rules over the nations.
29 All the prosperous of the earth will eat and worship,
      All those who go down to the dust will bow before Him, Even he who cannot keep his soul alive.
30 Posterity will serve Him; It will be told of the Lord to the coming generation.
31 They will come and will declare His righteousness to a people who will be born,
      that He has performed it.

It was from this Psalm that our Lord Jesus quoted, as He was dying on the cross - His last scripture quoted, before His purpose on earth was accomplished. It probably was written by King David during his reign 1011 B.C. to 1004 B.C. The "A.D." was apparent even then. Don't you think?

Good Friday

Precious Group,

It's Good Friday. God's Good Friday. Jesus Christ's Good Friday. The Holy Spirit's Good Friday. It is a Holy Trinity Happening with all Three actively involved in the day.

This new understanding which I gained today absolutely revolutionized my way of thinking. All my life I've treated Good Friday as if I were going to a "pity party." And really, it wasn't Jesus that I pitied as much as myself. I could really get down into the "ONE-on-one" of the situation so that I could even visualize myself hammering in those nails. Lucy "did Christ in" mentally every Good Friday, for as long as I can remember. And with this act, there was pride, along with piety.

Even as a child, I remember wearing my church clothes to school so that I could be dismissed early to go to the Good Friday service. "I'm an Episcopalian and we observe all three hours of Christ's crucifixion." "You're going to go home and play?" "Oh, not me! I'm going to church to pray." I would always love sitting all the way in the back corner against the wall. I thought no one would really notice me, except as they were leaving the church – which, of course, I didn't do. Can you believe this self-righteous piety? Isn't it just sickening? I mean "move over, Pharisees, and make room for me!"

So today, I must confess that I was right back in my corner viewing spot. I was ready to get into the absolutely horrendous horror of it all and I had my bag of "mental nails" ready to start hammering. But my load was lighter this year because of last night's Maundy Thursday

"Garden Party." Such a festival had not afforded my usual Good Friday mental "black funk" to settle in, for the blossoms and the prayers still permeated my mind.

The service began with Holy Communion, using the consecrated elements left from last night's service, for there is no consecration performed on Good Friday or Holy Saturday. I didn't know that and was told by Father Russell that this practice began early on, in the very first centuries, to set these two days apart. A real gash in time, don't you think? You have our Lord instituting His Last Supper, and then, for the next two days with His arrest — His trial — His crucifixion — His burial — His descent into Hell — there is a gash in time.

But for the first time, I started this Holy Day observance with Holy Communion and it revolutionized the atmosphere for me. You cannot be prideful with Holy Communion. It just doesn't work. And you can't be a "pity party" if you're having Holy Communion. It's like trying to mix oil and water. They just don't mix. The Lord's Supper is a gift — a free-will gift of grace from our Lord. It is His love poured out and there is no way to get around it. So, for the first time on Good Friday, I had ears to really listen and eyes to really see and a heart to really absorb Christ.

For the first time my "ONE-on-one" experience was stretched to a more cosmic one. Father Russell gave a visual description of the well-known crucifixion painting done by Salvador Dali. The perspective is such that you feel as if Christ is looking down on the global world as He hangs from the cross. It changes the reality of Calvary to the "real" reality — it's cosmic reality.

For "the act" is so much larger than we can ever comprehend or imagine. We usually picture three crosses all lined up in a row. In fact, this very week, I've passed two identical sets which were planted in church yards. In both sets, Christ's middle cross had been painted gold. Somehow gold spray misses terribly. In fact, I think no more crucifix kits should be sold, for even Great Sequoia crosses wouldn't do the event justice. For to try to re-enact or represent that moment, when Christ conquered sin, is impossible.

And even to Dali's noble crucifixion representation, I'd like to add our Creator God and the Holy Spirit looking on. Every time I've seen the Trinity represented by a triangle or three concentric circles or a fleur-de-lis, they've been either embroidered or painted or forged in place. Father Russell mentioned that there were love dynamics — "a real dynamism" between the three-in-one, at all times. You mean that God the Father wasn't just looking on from a distance, but was actively loving His Son during the Crucifixion? Do you mean that the Holy Spirit was being the "Comforter" during the Crucifixion?" "Wow!"

Why isn't the Trinity represented in moving neon lights or like the moving water waves that you see in novelty shops? True, it would be tacky, but what a better representation of the actual dynamics going on between our Father God – our Saviour Son – our Holy Spirit.

The very idea of me trying to re-enact Good Friday, the Holy Trinity's Good Friday, by making it a tiny little ONE-on-one pity party with my Jesus. What an insult! I mean talk about minimalism!

Besides this "cosmic reality," I was given additional insights by Father Russell like, "a crucified person would be almost eye level to the spectators." Can you imagine Jesus looking eye-to-eye, face-to-face, heart-to-heart to His mother and His best friend? I cannot imagine the pain shared in that triangular glance. And if I can't comprehend that, then how can I possibly comprehend the dynamics shared between the Father and the Son and the Holy Spirit during the crucifixion. As I have admitted, I had so limited the scenario that there was no place for the Holy Trinity. In fact, I had not really considered them.

I was also told that **Psalm 22**, which our Lord quoted: "My God, my God, why hast Thou forsaken Me?" was commonly used as a psalm for the dying. It would have been totally appropriate and plausible for any dying person to proclaim these words. This wasn't a "black hole" rip away from His Father, but instead a declaration of faith – a positive declaration of faith.

Father Russell also added additional poignancy to Christ's first statement on the cross, "Father, forgive them; for they do not know what they are doing." **Luke 23:34**. He stated that these words would have been said when Christ's pain would have been the most intense – the most unbearable. I can imagine the weight of His Body caused His flesh to rip, as those nails held. And what does our Jesus the Christ cry out for as His threshold of pain is splintered? He calls for pity on us – "Father, forgive them; for they do not know what they are doing." (Do we ever?)

I used to see Good Friday as strictly a "One-Man Show," which I would observe and even feel like I could put my two cents in to start the ball rolling or at least the hammer hammering.

I used to see God as only sitting back and observing and saying, "Not yet, Son." In Gethsemane, as His Son prayed for "release from this cup," He'd respond – "Not yet, Son." On the cross – He'd respond – "Not yet, Son." with the first agony. And I didn't even consider the Holy Spirit's role in the day.

Today I learned, and I hope I will always remember, that this wasn't a "One-Man Show," but rather a "Three-Ring Trinity Circus" performed by the Father, the Son, and the Holy Spirit.

It was a Holy Trinity Happening in which all Three were totally involved and each totally participated. It wasn't "ONE-on-one," Jesus and me. It's so much larger — so much more expansive — so much more cosmic. We cannot even comprehend the love flowing between the Three Rings, just so that the peanut gallery could become a part of the act once more.

"Dynamic Dynamism" as Father Russell called these Trinity Cosmic Dimensions. I'd call it the "Greatest Show on Earth or the Cosmos." Now I finally understand why it's called Good Friday!

Your sister in Christ,

Lucy

Holy Saturday

Precious Group,

Today we added lilies to the garden. You remember that garden created on Maundy Thursday in the chapel, that "Gethsemane Garden?" Everything now has been prepared for tomorrow. Lilies have been placed in each window, over the hymn boards, on the altar and even in the hands of the wooden chapel angels. There must have been eight of us "busy bees" scurrying around. You could feel the excitement.

We were all thrilled to be a part of the preparation, but how very different from the preparations made by Mary and Martha on that first Holy Saturday. Can you imagine their pain, their sorrow, their heartache that they had experienced the day before? They had watched their Lord die — slowly die — agonizingly die. The Man whom they loved more than life itself, because He had loved them — totally loved them — just as they were. But now He was gone. How could you go on, for The Light had gone out of the world. But duty called. They knew they must at least gather up the herbs and linen cloth needed to prepare their Rabboni's precious body. Of course, they couldn't do it yet, for it was still the Sabbath and a dead body could not be touched on Holy Days — even this precious body. But at least they could start collecting the necessary supplies so that the body could be prepared properly for burial. It had been so hastily done the day before. His body had almost been thrown into the tomb. His wounds hadn't been washed properly. Oh, those wounds — created by the nails, the whips, the sword and the thorns. How could they tear His body like they did, His innocent body? At least now He's out of His misery. They thought they never would be free of their own torment. Tomorrow, they could go to the tomb — at first light.

Today, we prepared the lilies, while they prepared with herbs and linen. Today, we prepared with a Holy Saturday service. Holy Scripture from the Prophets was read and we renewed our own baptismal vows and participated in the baptizing of two precious children.

What a comfort it was to walk through time with the Prophets, to the acts of God in the Old Testament, to fine-tune the reality of His presence throughout the ages. And I hoped that His disciples and closest followers did that on the first Holy Saturday. I'm sure they cried. I'm sure they were ashamed of their Good Friday fear flights. But possibly by the day after, they had gathered enough nerve to regroup, to assemble so that they could make plans – but there would be no plans – He was gone. To assemble so that they could review all the actions that had gone wrong – but there would be no review – He was gone. To assemble so that they could comfort and console each other in their disillusionment – but there would be no comfort or consolation – He was gone. Possibly one of them read the Holy Scripture aloud, read what the Prophets said – read what the Torah said. And maybe, just maybe, a spark was felt by a few of the desolated. And maybe, just maybe, some thought there could be more to the story. Maybe one of them said, "Listen to what the Holy Scripture says and do you remember those statements which Jesus made, which we didn't understand? Maybe, just maybe – there's more.

All day long, I saw preparations being made. At church, we prepared by placing lilies, renewing our baptismal vows, and baptizing. At a home I passed, children were preparing by hanging plastic eggs as high as they could reach, on a tree. At the lake, a mallard hen prepared by sitting on her nest located right next to a picture window. (What a joy to find.)

On the first Holy Saturday, there might have been a slight glimmer of the events to come, but most were probably still thinking of the death. Mary and Martha were preparing for a proper burial tomorrow – and thinking about the death. Whereas, we, the "Resurrection People," have the total picture – know the outcome of the story.

There's a lot more joy in our preparations. Why, even the way that mama duck is proudly and calmly sitting on her nest as a storm rages all around her, it seems that she knows – "just wait 'til tomorrow" – for at first light the Light Shines Once More.

Until tomorrow...

Your sister in Christ,

Lucy

Precious Group,

"Alleluia. Christ is risen.

The Lord is risen indeed. Alleluia."

This has been our proclamation for our almost two-millennia history. This is the statement that sets us apart. If we had to reduce our creeds down to one sentence or even just three words, it would have to read, "Christ is risen." It is this mind-set that makes us, His Church, a peculiar people, a set-apart people, a "Resurrection People."

Today, as no other day in the year, the "Resurrection People" gathered in full force, throughout all the world. There were Alleluia's proclaimed at each new dawning on this planet. Minute by minute, as the dawn marched around the earth, it was greeted by "Alleluia. Christ is risen. The Lord is risen indeed. Alleluia." Wouldn't it have been wonderful if there had been a universal recording made of this progressive proclamation? The rooster's crow which had once marked a dawn and a triple betrayal by Simon Peter, would have been deafened by this multitudinous declaration — all of our voices, joined as one, united in our Lord's victory over death and sin. On second thought, Peter's betrayals and our own betrayals had and have been cancelled by "the Event" of the day, not by the decibels of our sound.

I cannot tell you how thrilling it was to march into our church singing "Jesus Christ is Risen Today." It was absolutely fantastic — goosebump thrilling! There were trumpets and organ and kettle-drum rolls. These sound explosions painted a visual picture of that stone being rolled away. We, the church, were united in purpose as we should have been — to raise the rafters with the Easter proclamation of our reigning risen Lord. And we did a grand job!

To make the 7:00 a.m. service, I left the lake at 4:45. I had quietly gotten up, even before the alarm clock had gone off, gotten dressed, tiptoed down the stairs and out the front door. I had less than 4 hours of sleep, but I wasn't tired. I was invigorated by the anticipation of the Easter services. In total darkness, I drove, leaving my sleeping family and an alarm clock that I had forgotten to turn off. (Sorry, Winton.) My car companion was the voice of a Mr. Kelloge, on the radio. I felt like he had especially chosen Easter meditations and Easter music just for me. My heart was singing as I drove down the winding dirt road to the highway. My rejoicing became audible when a Mr. Bunny Rabbit hopped across my path. I burst into laughter and an "Alleluia. Christ is risen," sprang forth. You see, Mary Barwick had already given me "the Easter painting" as she saw it, which was a precious bunny with a garland of flowers around its neck. I loved the painting the moment I saw it, but couldn't imagine rabbits being part of my Easter Vigil — little did I know. For as the day continued, so did my rabbit rendezvous.

In the city, in the afternoon, I delivered precious letters to family members and rabbits kept crossing my trail, and then driving back to the lake, our paths continued to pass. It really got to be funny.

All right, I finally had to admit, rabbits, real rabbits, are part of the reality of this Easter. I myself was celebrating my 20th anniversary as the designated Blount Family Easter Bunny, not because of my skills, but rather, my being the sucker. But in all those years and the ones prior, I didn't recall the real thing being present. So what does a rabbit really have to do with this Easter? All that comes to mind is that, in each instance, it was an alone encounter with an alone rabbit. A "ONE-on-one" encounter which each time resulted in a mental dead halt and a verbal exclamation of "Alleluia." Each time I was going about, doing my own thing, minding my own business and checking off my own list — then, wham! the rabbit invasion would cause me to instantly start worshipping — "ONE-on-one." "Alleluia. Christ is risen."

As you've probably noticed, I've used this "ONE-on-one" image before. I don't know why, but for me, it visually vividly captures that "God and me," "God and you" relationship — that personal-unique relationship, which is so very important. It's not only important, but absolutely essential. I love group prayer, group Bible study, group singing and group worship. It thrills me every time I can gather with the church — the Universal Church — at any location, but preferably, of course, with the little flock on Clanton Street. To gather and celebrate His Holy communion, just fills in all my cracks and all my brokenness. But even more importantly, I believe that God wants that "ONE-on-one" daily communion — just Him and me — alone. It took me a long time to get to that realization. For years, I constantly slammed the door in His face. I would run busily away. Of course, I made my excuses... "Lord, I'm just not ready yet, for I'm not worthy. I'm a really big sinner. Why, let me show you my list just to back up this statement. See! Now, please give it back to me and I'll work on it. Maybe I can get it down a little, drop a few of them, so I can come back and visit with You in a little while. And I promise, I'll see you on Sunday, with my church group. OK? Isn't that enough?"

As the years passed, much to my surprise, I realized my sin list was getting longer, instead of shorter. In fact, it became obvious to me that it was a no-win situation. Lucy couldn't fix it, only Christ could. He wanted my list and He wanted me — totally. Not just on Sundays, but Mondays and Tuesdays and Wednesdays and Thursdays and Fridays and Saturdays — He wanted me totally, little old broken, sinful me — totally. A "ONE-on-one" relationship — a "ONE-on-one" joy dance — just between us two — just between you two.

It says throughout the Bible that we're dealing with a jealous, loving God. And I'm so glad.

Bunny for an angel.

Mary Barwick

I'm so glad that He wants little old broken me, just as I am, even more than I want Him – absolutely amazing! I don't understand it. If I were in charge, which I've unsuccessfully tried to be, I'd be a lot more selective. I'd only associate with the cream of the crop, but our Creator God wants a personal relationship with each one of His children. He wants to personally commune with every single one of us.

Besides using my sinners excuse to block communication, I'd also use the "poor, pitiful worshippers" excuse. "Lord, I need to read a few more books on prayer, before I start practicing. I need to attend a few more Bible classes, before I start regularly reading. I need to memorize a few more songs, before I start singing and praising."

Obviously, I was door slamming once more and as time marched on, I realized, with a lot of help from the "Helper," the Holy Spirit, that I'd never perfect these skills. That's why we are promised that He will meet us wherever we are, at whatever level – whether in a valley or on a mountaintop or on a fertile plain or in a dry desert. If we leave the door open and just say – "Lord, it's me. I'm here. I love You." – that's enough. Or even if we can just say "Lord," with a bent heart, I think that's enough. I believe He is – He is risen and He wants us – "ONE-on-one" for a dance.

For me, the very best illustration of this "ONE-on-one" relationship is found in **John 20:16**. Two words, only two "recognition" words were spoken on this first Easter morning, but they were totally sufficient. Nothing more needed to be said. – "Mary" – "Rabboni" – their dance continued.

On this Easter Day, I believe that it is imperative that each one of us not only take up our own individual crosses, designed especially with us in mind and follow Him, but it seems to be even more important, in fact absolutely essential, that we call out His Name, personally, not just in chorus, as a group exercise, but also on a "ONE-on-one," first-name basis. He already knows each of our names. Today, it's our turn to speak out and recognize Him!

"Alleluia. Christ is risen.

The Lord is risen indeed. Alleluia."

"Lord, it's me, Lucy. I'd like to introduce you to my friends. I know you're already on first-name basis with each one of us. Would you like us to individually call out Your Name so that the dance can continue?" "Oh yes, today, if you don't mind, I'd like to do the "Bunny Hop." You see, I've been running into these rabbits all day long and I like how they "Two Step."

Your "dancing fool" sister in Christ,

Lucy

Precious, Precious Group,

I am sitting in the choir stall of the church where I was raised, St. Mary's on-the-Highlands in Birmingham, Alabama. I'm all alone, except for His Presence. My Lord God's Presence surrounds me. The church seems so much smaller than I remembered. But the windows, ah, the windows are the most glorious stained glass imaginable. They are three times as big as I recalled! It's like you are engulfed by a picture-book New Testament, for they give you a breathtaking 360-degree panoramic view of our Lord's life. And in my mind, it could not be more perfectly executed.

Even their sequence and placement are significant to me. I'd never realized it before, but the first window you see when you enter is one of the smaller ones, but one of the most powerful. It's over the altar and depicts our Lord's Supper. As a child, I remember coloring a picture of this window while my mama did altar duty. I remember being so proud of getting the colors just right and staying in the lines. It was this window that greeted me every time I entered with my family or entered with the Junior Choir or entered with my Sunday School classes or entered with my Confirmation Class or entered to have three of my children baptized or entered to attend my brother's and my father's funeral. Your eyes gazed on hospitality – His hospitality in every situation. You and Christ seated in the middle of His twelve disciples and you felt that you were just an extension of the Supper going on. You felt not only invited, but welcomed, and I felt at home looking at this window. But the one that unexpectedly takes my breath away today, that has the biggest impact for me today, is the Ascension Window at the rear of the church. It is huge, the largest window of all. I cannot get over its magnitude and power. Perhaps it is the actual size that bowls me over. Perhaps I have become accustomed to the smaller version at the Church of the Ascension, which is over our altar. Perhaps it is the time of year – with Easter still clinging in the air, having taken place just five days previously. Or perhaps it is because of last night's prayer vigil at my own church.

Three friends met and prayed and sang and shared with each other and our Lord our concerns over a precious, precious fellow parishioner who was very sick. We gathered because one had called and you could hear the pain and tears in her voice. "What can we do?" "We can gather and comfort and pray." And that's just what we did.

We arrived at the church and greeted each other with hugs and then went to the chapel. And there on our knees, we talked to each other and then to our God. It was dark outside and at first, we felt that darkness in our spirits. The chapel has the only window in the church which allows you to see outside, for the rest of the windows are stained glass. And I am so glad for this clarity, for so often my mood has matched the amount of light which shines through that window. Especially this Easter week, for every morning, we had celebrated Morning Prayer and Holy Communion at 7:00 a.m. and the light through the window was almost blinding. It was like, "move over people, a new day is shining and remember, our Risen Lord reigns." Right under the window hangs the Easter lily arrangement that I made last Holy Saturday. Each morning I gave it a critique from the first day of "Lucy, it's gorgeous! Thank You, Lord," to daily counting the wilted flowers. By Thursday morning, I thought, it won't make it another day. I really should take it apart and throw it away. But I didn't and I'm so glad I didn't, for on this dark Thursday night, it shone brightly.

For as I said, it was dark in our world, but as we prayed and talked and sang, the gloom seemed to lift. Someone mentioned how the ceiling light was shining on one particular lily right in the middle of the arrangement and sure enough, it was. That Easter lily shone in the darkness like no other and the gloom was lifting.

At first, I burdened these ladies heavily by sharing the image of the statue of a man with his heart ripped out, located in Rotterdam. I've only seen the statue once, about twelve years ago. I don't even know if my mental picture matches the original, but what I recall, is a huge man with his arms held high above his head, with anguish on his face, as if he is screaming, silently screaming. And there, where his heart should be, is a hole, a huge empty gaping hole where his heart has been ripped out. It commemorates the bombing of the city during World War II. It also visually captures for me heart-ripping experiences.

I didn't have to explain its impact on me or what it meant. We three were mature ladies and part of life's maturing process includes heart-ripping episodes. For me, this statue captured the moment, but let me say, it was just a moment, a brief moment, not a frozen moment in time like the statue seemed to represent, for we are "Resurrection People," not "Rotterdam People."

In our darkness there is always the "Easter lily" reality. The dark chapel window with the one lily shining in our midst, was a more appropriate representation than the silently screaming man. For in our darkness, there is always the Light of Jesus Christ – our Lord and Savior's Light. He pierces the darkness, penetrates it with such force that we are only allowed brief moments of darkness. I'm occasionally accused of being a "Pollyanna type" and that really bugs me! For in that statement, one is directly saying one thing, but indirectly meaning, "Lucy, you're just in an 'ivory tower' and the reality of the world is not affecting you!" I beg to differ with the accuser's accusation and his or her perception of reality. I question what type of "Tower of London" prison they are occupying, for we are "Resurrection People," which means that in the fires and hot spots of life, we have our Lord.

Romans 8:28 says, "And we know that God causes all things to work together for good to those who love God, to those who are called according to His purpose."

I believe that with every fiber of my being. I've experienced that reality. I've had heart-ripping moments which have been healed by the Light — His Light infusing the situation and no prison bars or towers can keep out that Light.

Pollyanna? No! But a peculiar people — a set-apart people — a Resurrection People, Yes! As St. Paul said and as an enlightened Easter lily reminded me: "For I am convinced that neither death, nor life, nor angels, nor principalities, nor things present, nor things to come, nor powers, nor height, nor depth, nor any other created thing shall be able to separate us from the love of God, which is in Christ Jesus our Lord." **Romans 8:38-39**.

And Jesus said in the "Beatitudes:"

"Blessed are the poor in spirit, for theirs is the kingdom of heaven.
Blessed are those who mourn, for they shall be comforted.
Blessed are the gentle, for they shall inherit the earth.
Blessed are those who hunger and thirst for righteousness, for they shall be satisfied.
Blessed are the merciful, for they shall receive mercy.
Blessed are the pure in heart, for they shall see God.
Blessed are the peacemakers, for they shall be called sons of God.
Blessed are those who have been persecuted for righteousness, for theirs is the kingdom of heaven.
Blessed are you when men cast insults at you and persecute you,
    and say all kinds of evil against you falsely, on account of Me.
Rejoice, and be glad, for your reward in heaven is great,
    for so they persecuted the prophets who were before you."

That covers about all the "dark spot" possibilities, don't you think? Jesus is a Man of His Word. In fact, He is the "Word Made Flesh" and He covered them all with His Life. He put a new "Light" on all human experiences — His Light — where there is no darkness.

"Hello, my name is Lucy, which means 'light,' not 'Pollyanna.' And what is your neon name, your Christian name? I'm sure it's a bright one, too, for we are 'children of the Light.'"

Glow, people, glow. Darkness is only momentary.
Your Lit-up Lucy — lit up by His Light!

Dearest Precious Group,

"I think I can – I think I can – I think I can" – quoting the famous *Little Engine That Could*. We're getting ready to come around the bend and conclude this wonderful adventure. It's 7:00 a.m. and I'm sitting outside the Washington National Cathedral. I've known for about a month that your last letter, number 52, would be written here. I didn't know when, but I knew where.

And sure enough, here I am. Winton had a meeting scheduled at this location for over a year and guess where our hotel just happens to be? In walking distance to you-know-where – walking distance! Can you believe it? I've stayed in this city over 50 times, but never this near to the cathedral. Maybe I should start writing in iambic pentameter again, for the "Ah Ha's" keep pouring in!

Like yesterday, after going to Episcopal High School to check on the six small altar windows being given in honor of Winton, each one representing a member of our family, (Shh! Don't tell! It's a surprise!) I called the cathedral and asked what time they opened. I was informed that there was a 7:30 Holy Eucharist held in the Bethlehem Chapel. "Where?" "The Bethlehem Chapel." "Yes! I've got to be there!" I thought I was to write this letter in the Resurrection Chapel, but no, we're starting at the beginning with the Nativity, just as the letters started five months ago.

"Come long expected Jesus, born to set Thy people free." The birth – His Birth – the God-infused event that revolutionized the world – that brought us back into the reality of our original possibilities – the sinless possibilities, meant for us to experience – the relationship meant for us to experience – a personal relationship with our Almighty God. Because of this birthing, this grace-filled gift of Almighty God, we can be in fellowship with our Lord once more.

This chapel is lovely. It's all white marble. It's cool and pristine and quiet. It is in this type atmosphere that our Lord Jesus should have been born, surrounded by beauty, not cattle and a cave. But on second thought, He was coming to save us, the fallen. Beauty would have to come later, much later, after the mission – His Mission was accomplished.

Even in this chapel, I see His future being depicted over the altar. There is a breathtaking depiction of Mary and Baby Jesus, surrounded by angels. The marble carving is so strong that it made an impression on my heart. Over the carved reredos continuing to the ceiling, our little marble-arched windows. In three of the windows, possibly used only for structural support, are iron crosses. These little iron cross supports, situated right over the Nativity bas-relief, stuck and struck me just as powerfully as the "stone-birthing" depiction. Calvary was there from the beginning. And the artisan didn't stop with the usual cross-bar support system, but added a fleur-de-lis at the top. The cross top splintered into a fleur-de-lis. The cross bloomed into the Holy Trinity. Wow!

Are you thinking, "Lucy, you must be seeing things! You'll soon be turning nuts and bolts into icons." And you might be right, but so what? One of the most fun by-products of these letter writings to you, is each day I've been waking up with anticipation. My eyes have been retrained to look daily for the unexpected – the surprises and joys, that I might run into. Daily, I've risen and said, with meaning, "Lord, thank you for this day. May I be aware of what you would have me see. May I be aware of Your Presence, which surrounds me – in the places where you would have me go." I mean, I've been present – daily present – expectantly present – waiting for the joy to appear, so that I could share it with you.

And I'm going to miss you. Really miss you! I know some of you intimately, others I will never meet until this journey, this pilgrimage has ended. I don't know where the ripples of this little written rock will disseminate. And it doesn't matter. It really doesn't matter, as long as it is used to His Glory.

I did want you to know that there's already a little monument placed so that our letter talks won't be forgotten. It's in our bathroom. Sorry about the location, but really it is a pretty bathroom and one location that I visit daily. (Lucy, hush.) Anyway, about the same time I started writing you, I bought a jewelry box for about $20 at the Farmer's Market. It is ingenious! It's wooden and looks like a miniature garden gazebo. Its roof comes off and the stairs pull out, for you to store your jewels. That's fun in itself, but the feature which really sold me was the swing. For right in the middle hangs a little working two-seater porch swing. And I have a real weakness for such havens. Growing up, I spent hours in my grandmother's porch swing with my first cousin, Dorothy. We became so good at operating the motion, that we could both lie down at the same time, facing opposite directions and each use a leg to push on the chains, to keep the momentum going. In fact, we would sometimes get so carried away that we would hit the house wall and bring my grandmother flying out to scold. "We're sorry, we won't do it again" – really meaning, not in the next couple of minutes. We would talk fast, fast, fast and then throw in a "Boy, I'm bored!" and then continue our entertaining conversations.

This jewelry box will be a constant reminder for me, not only of the long ago talks with Dorothy, but even more, our delightful sojourn together. This little wooden replica was made by one of the inmates at Kilby Prison. This box represented for me, in a beautiful and meaningful way – freedom. The freedom to share our lives with one another in the comfort of a little swing or in the comfort of a little letter. And when our friend is not sitting there with us and these letters cease, we always have our Eternal Friend as our companion. That is a great comfort to me, in fact, the greatest comfort to me. He is present at all times, in all situations. We are never alone. We always have a "swing-Mate" for this ride.

Now let's go visit the next chapel, it's just down the hall. As I leave the Bethlehem Chapel, I look up and over the door is carved, "He shall save His people from their sins," – Yes, Lord. As I approach the St. Joseph of Arimathea Chapel, there is a loud roar coming from the tomb. And that's exactly what this chapel feels like – a tomb. It is a foundational chapel, for its four columns, each 27 feet in diameter, support the bell tower, with its 900 tons of masonry and 120 tons of bells. This chapel is located right below the cathedral's crossing and is at the deepest elevation. There are no windows, only a gold, red, black and white painting behind the altar. It depicts the processional to the tomb. The three crosses are on the left and there is a frozen visual march to Joseph of Arimathea's tomb. Jesus lies pale and lifeless in the middle, surrounded by loved ones.

A heavy subject matter, but one lightened by the gold paint shot throughout the picture, plus the light giggles and laughs of the Beauvoir School's first graders. Their sounds made the "tomb room" into a "joy box." These precious children were the cause of the earlier roar I'd heard. They were putting on an "Earth Day Pageant" for their parents. It was adorable, with singing and reciting and praying. "Earth Day" in the "Tomb Room," next to the ashes columbarium where Helen Keller and her teacher, Ann Sullivan are interred along with about 200 others. Isn't that grand? How very appropriate! There's no gloom in this room, only 100 six-year-olds, wearing their own handmade T-shirts and their proud parents, celebrating the earth, God's earth, in a room which commemorates the gift of some earth given 2000 years ago for a tomb.

Now, across the hall, I entered the Resurrection Chapel. It is here that we will end. I wish so much that it was quiet! There are three ladies busily arranging flowers on the altar. Yea! Two leave! Now there's only one lone laborer, using lilies and iris and snapdragon to create a floral fan. This is not my favorite shape and a real "no, no" in Sheila McQueen's arrangement manual, but here it's just fine, for the arrow points straight up to our Resurrected Christ.

I'm writing to you on my knees, not out of piety, but out of sheer awe. I am surrounded by the most unbelievable golden mosaics. There are seven of them, each depicting the various appearances of our Resurrected Lord before His Ascension. When you look at them, they almost hurt your eyes. The colors are so vivid. And I am so glad that this is the way the artist decided to try and attempt to recapture the uncapturable.

All aboard!   Mary Barwick

Can you imagine the reality of these events? Can you imagine the first sighting made of our Resurrected Christ and then trying to transfer and translate that experience to others? "My Lord Has Risen!" Words can't capture the moments — neither can mosaics, but they come mighty close, a noble effort has been made. For while you remain kneeling and gazing, you know that the biggest "Ah Ha," the "Cosmic Miracle," is trying to be recaptured and represented. There is enough holiness in this room, exuding from these miracle mosaics to at least solicit a reverent "yes" — "YES!" My Lord is Risen!

This was the same response I felt two days ago, at the "Easter" funeral of Dexter. He was the precious, gentle young man, godly young man, that I mentioned in our last letter. He died on the second Easter Sunday. His funeral was the most glorious celebration of a life that I have experienced. The hymns were Easter hymns. The flowers were Easter flowers, with more color. The congregation was united in one feeling. The acknowledgment that this was a godly young man was so strong that you could feel the walls of the church and the walls of time, giving way to a God Expanse. You knew, beyond a doubt, that our Lord God is Risen, just as these mosaics depict, and you knew and know that Dexter is now a part of that reality — totally a part of that reality.

The older I get, the smaller I seem to be. For it seems that all of our previous happenings are so minute in the overall scheme of things. The walls of time seem to be coming down and the view of the big picture, God's big picture on which we are only a tiny spot in time, seems to be coming more in focus. Dexter has made the time change from this tiny present reality to the Godly infinite reality. Again, you can't capture the truth in words or mosaics or Easter hymns or Easter flowers — you just know.

The scripture that Dexter claimed as his own was **Philippians 4:13**, "I can do all things through Christ Who strengthens me." "I can" — "I can" — "I can" — "do all things through Christ Who strengthens me!" May this also be our battle cry — until we join the expanse — the Total Expanse of our Risen Lord. He reigns! Precious Group. He reigns!

Our individual pilgrimages continue. I've enjoyed our short walk together and look forward to the future — His Future.

> Love and till we meet again,
> I am your sister in Christ Jesus, our Lord,
> Lucy

P.S. I hope you will now go write a letter to your own precious group. It's fun and they're not graded for grammar, just treasured with love.

Precious Group, Let's Go Deeper

Precious Group,

"Emergency! Charles is locked in the bathroom. He can't get out!" Spontaneous laughter bubbles up from the group on the bus. It feels so good, for it relieves some of my pent-up pain. I've felt like I had a stake slowly hammered into my heart, for yesterday I partook of the Oberammergau Passion Play....

But first, I'd like to begin our visit in a different way, if you don't mind, for I need to get a few things out. Before leaving on this trip with my mother and sister, Prim Brown asked, "There will be a letter, won't there?" And that was a very heavy gauntlet thrown down and I didn't know if I would or could pick it up. After completing the original 52 *Letters to the Precious Group*, the "still space" has been important and necessary, for the book left me drained. It has been a wonderful emptiness – like, "There, we've done it!" – and I didn't know if I was quite ready to give up this calm – but here goes!

As you know, I like to put words together. Winton usually says, "There's no such thing!" And he's right, but they do paint pictures, don't you think? Two words that have been growing together in my mind over the last few months are "womb room." That's right – "womb room." We all started together. Our God created existence in such a space. As mothers, we have the privilege of being allowed the baby blues after our "womb room" has been vacated. And then we try to recreate and reflect this space in our homes, where our families are nurtured.

And alas, again as mothers, we have the privilege of being allowed to have the empty nest syndrome and that's where I am right now. After 20 years, my expanded "womb room" is empty, for my four children have moved out and off. Their rooms stay clean. There are no smelly shoes and socks in the TV room. There are no circle designs being made on the furniture by half-filled cans, bottles and glasses. I have uninterrupted nights of sleep. The windows aren't rattling from musical blasts. Doors aren't slammed. Bathroom time isn't invaded. I mean, my world is different!

Daisy the dog captures my mood perfectly. She has become a slug and it's not because of her continual weight problem, but from her lack of stimuli by the group. No balls thrown, no sock tug-of-war, no chase inside the house to see how many Oriental rugs can become magic carpets and move. Her world has drastically changed, too. I am allowing her this slug time. And, thank goodness, Winton is allowing me mine. (I know he misses them too, for football with Lucy isn't the same as football with the group!) And I do know that there is light at the end of the tunnel, just like the ones I've been experiencing all morning (mourning) long.

We're traveling by bus through Germany, Austria, Liechtenstein, and ending up in Lucerne, Switzerland. The tunnels are numerous (Augsburg tunnel – 8.8 miles). And isn't life like that – times when you don't know exactly where you're going or what's next? Your peripheral vision has been limited by the dark tunnel experience. You know you must go forward, even if at a snail's pace, and you know you can't go backwards. You don't know what's next – what exactly will be the next program or plan or event in your life. But you do know that forward you must go in order to leave space for the next. But there's a small voice inside saying, "No, I don't want to go forward. I know my old world. I know this 'womb room'." It's comfortable and secure and predictable, in kind of an unpredictable way. No, but we must move on. We must let go of the predictable so that we can expand toward God's profound.

Our tour guide just said, "Every summit of every mountain in the Alps has a cross on top." I wonder why not in all these tunnels? That's where I'd like to plant them, or to distribute them at the entrances. "Ladies and gentlemen, you're getting to go through a 'tunnel experience.' You may travel at your own pace. It's single file, please, and here's a cross to lighten (illumine and unburden) your passage."

Back to the Passion Play – yes – today I went single file through a five-and-a-half-hour tunnel. I believe that this experience will be non-transferable, but I'll try. What comes to mind, again, is a stake slowly being hammered into my heart. For five and a half hours – two and a half hours in the morning, three hours in the afternoon – over 1000 Oberammergau residents reenacted the Redemptive Life of our Savior. This small community of 5500 has been faithfully recreating this play every ten years since 1633. In that year, a vow was made to God that if the community was spared from the ravages of the Black Plague, the residents, in thanksgiving, would perform the Passion Play.

And so it continues, with 98 performances in 1990, each consisting of 14 acts and each act utilizing three different modes of action for the storyline. It is sung by a 50-member, white-robed chorus which periodically files on and off the stage; or told through "frozen stills," where the villagers recreate a Biblical scene in total frozenness; or the third mode, typical stage drama. It's all in German. So you follow along in a 200-page translation. Grand opera becomes like a Saturday morning cartoon show when compared to the Passion Play.

Often I wanted to scream. I did not think I could take much more. For me, the stills were the most powerful. To see examples of some of man's evil frozen still was personally condemning, almost crucifying.

To personally have to say each word in your mind in order to understand the play – again, made it more personally piercing. To have to hear the hammer hammering, to have to see the blood flowing from each wound, the spear piercing the side, an actual limp body being lowered from the cross and then cradled in the mother's arms; – "God" – "I can't take any more!" – "Forgive me!" – was the screaming in my heart – "Forgive me!" – "I crucify you daily!"

Thank the dear Lord, in the last scene all join forces. There are the chorus and some of the players, mainly children, and the final still – the Resurrected Christ standing in glory – and slowly, for the first time, the villagers walk into the still. They join their Messiah. The still becomes an alive reality – our alive reality. The audience started clapping and then I stood, along with many, and wished that I could walk into this "Redemptive Still," too. But we are, aren't we really? Daily we walk in it, towards it.

I mean, these tunnels, these passages we are in are really marches forward to the ultimate womb room – the Redemptive Reality of our Christ. Don't you think?

"Emergency! Charles is locked in the bathroom! He can't get out!" Spontaneous laughter bubbles up.

"Emergency! Lucy is stuck in a tunnel! She can't get out!" Spontaneous laughter bubbles up. "Oh yes I can! My womb room is a lot bigger than I realized and it's not a still-life – a frozen scene – but rather a 'Resurrection adventure'.

"Lord, I am grieved by your crucifixion. Yesterday my heart was pierced deeper into the reality of my own personal responsibility. This is not a frozen reality, but a redemptive reality. I'm ready to go forward now with your cross as my guide.

"But before we take off, would you mind if I throw Daisy a ball? You see, she's been a little sluggish lately, for she's been missing....

"Oh, I forgot – You also have missed, and do miss, and will continue to miss... You understand.

"My Lord, let's get going and we can speed up a little, if you'd like. Will you hold my hand? I don't know the way, but then – You do! – Alleluia!"

Your sister in Christ,
Lucy

Precious Group,

"Has anyone told you you're looking pretty today?"

"Goodness, you sure are spreading joy around!"

"Well, I just thought someone should tell you."

I wanted to continue this enchanting conversation with this older, mysterious man (notice I didn't say tall, dark and handsome), but he was seated right behind me on the plane and it would have been a little awkward to just turn around and say, "Hi! Let's talk!" I mean, it's all right for a two-year-old to stand up in her airplane seat and talk to the person seated behind them. It's expected behavior, right? But somehow, it's not for a 42-year-old. So I just had to stay strapped in and restrained and will have a written dialogue with you instead of a vocal one with him. Plus, my mama told me, "Never talk to strangers."

So here goes. What I'd like to say to the mysterious man via you, is "thanks." Thank you for giving me an unexpected little joy gift that lightened my day, but more importantly, reminded me of who I am — a precious child of God — a joy giver — at least, that is what I should be when I'm plugged in with my Maker; when I am so tuned in with Him that His essence just seems to permeate the area. Don't get me wrong. It has nothing to do with Lucy, but with God!

At the Leaders' conference, one of the other groups gave their participants a little sachet of violets with the scripture **2 Corinthians 2:14** attached: "For we are to God the aroma of Christ among those who are being saved and those who are perishing." The mysterious man gave me a whiff of that aroma, which I had forgotten all about, for I'd been packing and pouting. I had organized my world, or at least kind of organized my world. I mean, I did what I could, considering I had left everything to the last minute. Do you know that kind of desperate organization, when you leave everything to the last minute so that your list of 20 "to do" items becomes a list of "dumped" items instead of "done," because you have run out of time? Well, this was my morning. I'd dumped everything except packing and felt proud that I'd at least accomplished that feat. And then I was bombarded with children's phone requests to bring warm clothes to Washington! How? And when? Didn't they know I'd already finished organizing and packing and I hadn't left any room for winter woolens for four (three children plus one girlfriend: Win, our oldest, was no longer in need, because with his wedding this summer also went his winter wardrobe.)

I was exasperated! I pulled out the humiliatingly huge duffel bag, the same one that I'd embarrassingly taken to Washington State. The same one that I'd have to pay the porter double to transport, in case he required a hernia operation from carrying it! I invaded three closets, grabbing and pulling and stuffing heavy clothes into this bag, all the while huffing and puffing and pouting. I mean, this was not a pretty picture! This was not the mother, the one who's been moaning and groaning because "the children are gone and I'm not needed anymore." I mean, I was bugged and I continued my buggedness all the way to the airport and all the way up the airplane ramp and all the way to my seat. I mean, I am sure that if my countenance was glowing by the time I ran into the mysterious man, it was not from my exposure to God, as in Moses' case, but rather from my agitated state of rush and rage!

"Has anyone told you you're looking pretty this morning?" What a wonderful whiff! "For we are to God the aroma of Christ among those who are being saved and those who are perishing." Lord, thank You! Lord, thank You for allowing this man to come along and bump me back into Your realm. How often I forget! How often, if my world isn't going just as planned — as I planned, not You planned, Lord — the old self-centered self surfaces. And gosh, if I get so tired of it, it must really be a burden to You!

I picture myself as one of Your dumber old sheep, going along, getting off the path and You, my Shepherd, taking the hook of Your staff and catching me around the neck and pulling me lovingly back. This act is required so often, I mean, daily, hourly, that it amazes me that I don't have whiplash!

But I've discovered possibly why I don't have this neck ailment. It's not just because of having a stiff neck, which my Lord knows about, but it's because of "recovery and discovery." These two words were given to me while on this family trip. Our main purpose was to attend the dedication of the Calloway Chapel at Episcopal High School in Alexandria, Virginia. This beautiful new sanctuary was named for a 96-year-old professor who had taught at The High School for over 70 years. His exemplary Christian life has influenced literally three generations of students.

And it was his comments — not the bishop's, nor the chaplain's, nor the headmaster's, nor the board chairman's, nor any of the other dignitaries' comments, but Mr. Calloway's comments — that blessed me and reminded me of why I don't have constant whiplash. He asked that the chapel always be open so that the students could always come for "recovery and discovery."

"Recovery and discovery." Aren't those two glorious words? When I'm going absolutely off the beaten track and the Lord Jesus gets His hooked staff around my neck and stops me dead in my tracks and pulls me back in and gently says, "This way, Lucy," I can "recover and discover." But it surely doesn't happen in the mad rush of things. It has to be in a place of solace, a place where my Lord God can get my undivided attention.

Often my "recovery and discovery" and refocusing and realigning with my Lord is done at the lake, but it can be unexpected places as well – in the chapel of my car – in a closet with the door shut – in an airplane with a mysterious stranger.

Lord, You've got my undivided attention! Right now! At this very moment! I love You! (I wonder what I'll fix Carol for supper?) Sorry Lord, I'm ready for Your crooked staff again – around the neck, please. It's just how I like it. Pull me in close, not for R&R time, not for rest and relaxation, but for R&D time – "recovery and discovery."

"For we are to God the aroma of Christ among those who are being saved and those who are perishing…." **2 Corinthians 2:14.**

How do we keep that aroma of Christ strong? By constantly being in that "recovery and discovery" mode. Find that place of solace where the Shepherd can pull you in, closer and closer….

To Him be the glory!

Your sister in Christ,

Lucy

Dec. 1

Precious Group,

I can't wait to get home today and go buy a B-dazzler. A what? A B-dazzler. Mary Barwick told me about this wonderful invention which allows you to sparkle up anything. I'm going to use it to transform nine bargain basement, hot pink shirts into designer creations. I know they're going to be fabulous, darling! The rhinestone cowboy will covet these duds!

Why am I going to do this? Don't worry, it's not going to be your Christmas present. Instead, it is going to be uniforms for the Rosettes. I know you haven't heard of the group yet, but just you wait! The plan is that "The Three Ladies of Morning Prayer" (we've been meeting Monday through Friday at 7:00 a.m. for over a year for this service) are getting ready to go out into the world.

Our first limited engagement will be at Father Purcell's Exceptional Center. Once a week, for two hours, we are going to put on sparkly shirts and rose perfume, take up our Cassio pianos and get on our hands and knees and pray and play with the children.

The music we're going to make and the tunes we're going to tap and rap might not be recognizable to the general audience, but I bet will be favorably received by the heavenly host. For you see, it says in **Luke 2:13:** "And suddenly there was with the angel a multitude of the heavenly host praising God, and saying, 'Glory to God in the highest and on earth peace, good will toward men.'" And not to be presumptuous on our part, but our methods of praising God are similar.

We'll weekly be praying in the Rainbow Room at Father Purcell's. Come catch our act sometimes or better yet, come join us. As I said, I bought nine shirts, not three, so room to grow.

Why am I telling you all of this? Am I just trying to get some free publicity? Well, not exactly. You see, the Word says, "Let your light so shine before men, that they may see your good works and glorify your Father which is in heaven." **Matthew 5:16.** As we three ladies have daily visited over coffee after morning prayer, one has shared her desire for children and one has shared her desire for volunteer work. The world's response would be, "Dream on, sisters, no way!" – for the first is not married and the second has been very sick and been told that volunteer work is out!

But wait a minute! Who says? Maybe society says, but what does our Savior say? "Let your light so shine before men, that they may see your good works and glorify your Father which is in heaven." **Matthew 5:16.** And I believe that everybody has "light" possibilities all of his life, not just during prime time. In fact, I know it! In the past, I've spent over three years at Father Purcell's and I have seen sparkles come from the least expected. Can't walk – can't talk – can't see – can't hear – but there's a shine, nevertheless, exuding from each one of these children.

For example, Jeremiah. For over a year, we would put a Cassio piano in front of him once a week and place his hands on it and press down on them, making a glorious dichotomy of sound, but with no apparent response from Jeremiah. Then one day – one glorious day – bang! Jeremiah himself struck the keys. It took thirty minutes for him to lower his hands and make contact with the keyboard – then – then away he went – Bang! Bang! Bang! His timing might have been off and his tune might not have been recognizable to some, but I guarantee the heavenly host clapped continuously!

Last week I asked one of the grand pillars of our church, "How does an Altar Guild member distribute the Healing Service Pamphlet during the service?" She answered "As a rule…" Goodness, I do believe we need to watch out for "As a rule…," for the limits, the stifling limits such a statement can produce can be devastating. It can snuff out "lights" and Jeremiahs and Rosettes everywhere!

So, ladies and gentlemen, watch out for those "As a rule…" statements. I'm not suggesting chaos, for our Lord God's world is an orderly one. Just be sure that the boundaries set and the rules followed are God-made, not man-made. For I believe ours can be a little limiting, whereas His can be expansive.

Mary Barwick told me about her little two-year-old nephew, Charlie, who went visiting the grazing bronze sheep at Alabama Shakespeare Festival. He took with him a swan feather which he had found. He then proceeded to tickle the sheep's ears, he said, "to make them laugh." You know, I bet they possibly did. If you allow the limits to let up a little bit — let up the man-made limits — who knows!

You can catch the first performance of the Rosettes Friday at 9:30 in the Rainbow Room at Father Purcell's. Our shirts will be B-dazzling and our perfume will be Roses and our music — well, it might be a little unorthodox, but I bet we'll get a standing ovation from afar!

And at this Christmas time, do yourself a favor and go buy a B-dazzler, too! Rhinestones help remind us of our real reflection — our Lord's reflection!

Your Rosette B-dazzling sister in Christ!

Lucy

Dec. 17

Precious Group,

Jud just bought a Stetson cowboy hat and it tickles my heart. Why? Because of the memories that it evokes. It reminds me of when he was twelve years old, which was the last year of his mother-centered babyhood. I'm sure that he sees his thirteenth year as a more memorable milestone (when full-blown puberty set in), but for me, twelve was the monumental mark. It was a glorious boy-man age, for there were still traces of the innocent child left. I'd still get an embarrassed or unexpected kiss or hug or giggle or cry. Even though I could see the man emerging, the baby boy was still present for a few moments, brief memorable moments.

And this new Stetson hat reminded me of such a time — Europe 1983 — the family trip. One month — eight countries — six of us traveling in a five-passenger car. We made the movie, *European Vacation*, seem meek and mild by comparison. Jud's designated seat in the car was the console. There he sat looking more like an elf than the littlest brother, for you see, he had purchased, with his own money, one of those green felt Alpine hats. He wore it morning, noon and night. All of us laughed at him and did a fair bit of teasing, but in no way did that affect the importance of the hat. It became fancier and fancier as the trip progressed, for with each new location, he added a city pin. And thus it became heavier and heavier with hat pins, and more and more hilarious.

And now, seven years later, here sitting on the sofa in Steamboat Springs, Colorado, is the big strapping nineteen-year-old with the Stetson and it tickles my heart. He's eating cereal, dressed in long underwear and the hat – a perfect morning outfit! Yes – the little boy lives once more!

He's not the only adorable boy I've seen on this spur-of-the-moment four-day skiing trip. Yesterday I went to St. Paul's Episcopal Church. It was small and intimate and alive and always a real treat to attend. The parishioners wear pants and parkas. The choir practices fifteen minutes before the service starts and anyone can join. The visitors receive a loaf of bread like the Communion loaf and a warm welcome. Children seemed to come and go all during the service and when a baby started crying during the sermon, the priest just mentioned the cute culprit's name, which instantly quieted him down. Then, when it came time for the lay reader to make announcements, the minister sat on the front pew and all of the children filed in for Communion and joined him on the bench. One angelic-looking young man, I'd guess about nine years old, boldly plopped himself down in the minister's lap. He was greeted with an affectionate hug. The boy then proudly turned to the little boy next to him and stuck out his tongue. I almost burst out laughing and it was another heart-tickle.

And then I started thinking about lap-sitting. I love the scripture when Jesus said, "Suffer the little children to come unto me for such is the kingdom of God." This beautifully intimate word picture has been portrayed with great tenderness over the ages, and justly so. You can just shut your eyes and envision our Savior encircled by children – beautiful, orderly, angelic children. Right? Wrong! I bet they were more like the little boy with the tongue sticking out, possibly pushing and shoving and embarrassing their parents to death. I mean, enthusiasm reigned. "Me first!" "Me first!" "Jesus, I love you!"

"But your hair's not combed!" "Your hands are dirty!" "You don't have on your Sunday best!" "You haven't confessed your sins!" "You're not perfect!" – might have been their parents' paralyzing responses.

But the children – onward and upward – into their Jesus' lap. And I bet He reached down and picked up each and every one of them, just as they were, and gave each and every one of them what they desired – an affectionate hug and a tender touch. And what about the little boy who stuck out his tongue? I bet Jesus would have burst out laughing and given him a special squeeze. Of course, He'd admonish him for the unkind act to his peer, but He would appreciate the unadulterated pleasure that the young boy was showing. "See, I'm here sitting in the lap of Someone who loves me – even if I stick out my tongue!" I mean, that's assurance, blessed assurance! Don't you think?

This Christmas season the song which keeps playing in my brain over and over again is the "Little Drummer Boy." It started a few weeks ago when I bought Mary Barwick's first granddaughter, Hannah, a "Little Drummer Boy" cross-stitched picture. It's pink and precious (both Hannah and the picture). But what I liked most about this representation was not just the picture, but more importantly the "Pah Rum Pah Pah Pum," outlining the whole scene. The song says, "I played my best for Him." It doesn't say how melodic that was or whether the grown-ups would have said, "Cut that noise out!" It just says, "I played my best for Him…." Isn't that grand? What a gift for the Christ!

I wish that there was a mall Santa who would just sit and give each visiting child a genuine hug – not asking about his or her yearly behavior or his or her wants, but instead, all each child would receive was a genuine hug.

I wish the children could bring drums and ballet slippers and tricycles and Big Wheels and roller skates and baseballs and soccer balls and Alpine hats – I mean, the ultimate show and tell possible. Each would "play my best for Him" and each would receive a genuine hug and each would understand a little bit better about Who's birthday it really is. Or maybe they already know. Maybe they remember the hug – His hug. Maybe we grown-ups have made the "Rum Pah Pah Pums" of Christmas out of tune.

Maybe there needs to be an "Adults Only" line for the hugging Santa. Maybe we're the ones who need to come with enthusiasm to the Christ this Christmas – with sticky hands and smudged noses and sins and Stetson hats – possibly pushing and shoving, but enthusiastically loving. Maybe we need the hugs and the heart-tickles this season.

May His Peace

    Pah Rum Pah Pah Pum

May His Joy

    Pah Rum Pah Pah Pum

May His Love

    Pah Rum Pah Pah Pum

Tickle your heart this Christmas!

    Your sister in Christ Jesus our Lord,

    Lucy XX

Dec. 28 – Jan. 1
LaQuinta, California
Gillionville, Georgia

Precious Group,

Did you receive any stringless presents this year? I'm not referring to those lacking ribbon, but rather to those having no strings attached — such as an unexpected gift or possibly an undeserved one.

While walking to breakfast this morning, I observed one of these delightful exchanges. There was this Shirley Temple-type three-year-old walking with her proud grandmother and they both stopped to receive ooohs and ahhhs of adoration from one of the hotel cleaning ladies. The woman had stopped dead in her tracks, stooped down, held out her arms and adored. The child walked right into the lady's outstretched arms and gave her a kiss. I think the proper grandparent was a little taken aback, for her flustered response was, "What is your name?" The employee answered, "Joyce." And then the grandmother said, "Joyce, you are chosen." In other words, "Not everybody receives a kiss from my adorable grandchild." And I'm sure she was right and Joyce did have reason to rejoice, for an unexpected kiss is about the best kind to receive. Don't you think? We all giggled or blushed at some time or another when this unexpected gift was given. We were embarrassed to death, but tickled pink. We turned red as a beet, but it made us feel "grrrreat, really grrrreat," for it did make us feel chosen.

All this Christmas week, one of the appointed Psalms for Morning Prayer was **Psalm 85** and the verse that I've loved most was Verse 10: "Mercy and truth have met together; Righteousness and peace have kissed each other."

I've closed my eyes and pictured the Virgin Mary holding her Baby, our Lord Jesus and giving Him His very first human kiss. "Mercy and truth have met together; Righteousness and peace have kissed each other." Seems to be a perfect verse to subtitle this scene, or better yet, "Wow!," as Nan Hobbs used last week at the Wednesday night service. "Wow!" What a grand word! It's perfect to use when we can't capture a situation. Teenagers have added some more grand wow words to our world: awesome, far out, radical, to the max. Such an expletive is a perfect response to a stringless present, for there's no way you can pay back such a gift. You can just humbly beam and enjoy and give rave reviews and cheers and wows.

Nan expanded my understanding of wow. She had been told by a friend that "Wow" would be her response when she got to heaven and asked all those hard questions of God, hard questions for us — of "Why, Lord?" "Why, Lord, did this happen and that happen?" All of those unanswered, horribly hard questions concerning those situations and circumstances that we've experienced personally or witnessed from afar that just didn't – with only our human comprehension – make sense. And Nan, who personally had already experienced one of those awful, incomprehensible aches, said that a friend told her that "Wow" would be her response when God shared with her the whole picture – His whole picture. His infinite wisdom and majesty will so dominate the scene that even the hardest, seemingly tragic scenarios will become clear with His Light and will be met by us with an all-out "Wow!"

And that's the word I've carried around all this Christmas season, thanks to Nan. When those glimpses of God's grand majesty have broken through – those stringless presents – an unexpected kiss given by a three-year-old – Wow! – a hummingbird drinking from a flower – Wow! – my children and their cousins acting out the nativity scene in our hotel room – Wow! – a New Year's Eve blue moon – Wow!

But the biggest wow I've experienced over this past week was not an example of the "grand" instantly breaking through, or at least it didn't seem so, but rather more like a Nan wow in which that response didn't take place until the full picture was seen. I visited a nearby church. Over the altar hung a huge crucifix. The church was in total darkness except for the side altars, so it took a little while for my eyes to adjust. And then slowly the representation of Christ crucified came more into focus. There He hung, heavily hung, for that scene always feels weighty on my heart. But this crucifix was different, for as my eyes adjusted to the darkness, I saw that Jesus' right arm was reaching down and enfolding a man or woman. Wow! My usual response of heavy-heartedness gave way to a weightless "Wow!" What a wonderful representation of Christ's love for us! And then I noticed on the left-hand side of the altar, on the floor, was a crèche scene where Mary and Joseph were adoring their Son.

The two scenes juxtaposed next to each other made the impact more meaningful. I know I can't capture it – even "Wow" doesn't really work. But try closing your eyes. Picture Mary giving her precious Baby His first kiss and Him responding. And then imagine Mary handing Him to you and you being able to give Him a kiss – "Wow!"

Then imagine Christ hanging from the cross in agony, dying, but nevertheless willing and able to reach down with one of His arms and giving you a hug – "Wow!"

We've each possibly been asked numerous times, "Is Jesus your personal Lord and Savior?," even possibly to the point that the question makes you feel a little uncomfortable or a little squeamish. I believe a kiss from a baby or a hug from the Crucified would make each one of us feel a little more relaxed with the reality of our "chosen-ness."

And what about those hard-to-answer stumbling-block-type questions? Relax – the answers will come – and I believe our responses will be "Wow!" Weightless "Wows!" for the ultimate no-strings-attached stringless gift has been given.

His life because of His love

for each one of us

individually

personally

"Wow!"

There's nothing we can do or say to earn or repay "The Gift," but we can adore like on that first Christmas when "Mercy and truth have met together: Righteousness and peace have kissed each other" – for all eternity.

May we keep counting those stringless presents daily, for they're good reminders of the Ultimate One. May we keep practicing those wow responses, for they remind us that our worldly woes aren't so weighty after all. They might seem heavy, but at some point those worldly old woes are going to give way to weightless "Wows!"

Now say that last paragraph three times and see if you don't start giggling and begin to feel a little lighter. We are, you know – light, I mean. He's already made us that way.

Joyce is chosen for she received a stringless present of a kiss from a three-year-old.

You and I are chosen too, for we have received the ultimate gift – His life!

Happy New Year!

This year, may we count the wows and not the woes.

This year, may we remember the woes never outweigh the wows.

This year, may we remember that we are lighter than we think!

…because of a stringless present given to us almost two thousand years ago.

Love,

Lucy

Jan. 5, Epiphany

Precious Group,

Right now I'm on a sofa sabbatical. I'm sitting Indian-style on my favorite couch at Lake Martin. It's my favorite because it's made just right for me. It's squashy and short. The back pillows can prop me up for writing or worship and prop me down for reading and sleeping. It's better than any recliner chair, both in looks and versatility, but best of all is the view. Its end is pushed right up against a plate-glass window that overlooks the lake, so I feel like I'm hanging over the water.

It's the second grey foggy day in a row and that's OK because it really matches my mood toward this New Year. In all of my forty-two years, I've never felt as unsure about the coming New Year and what it has in store. I'm not afraid or anxious, just a little wary. Most of you know we have a dear friend who has a brain tumor and most of you know his fourteen-year-old daughter, my godchild, is living with us – and then there's my grandmother who's ill and then there's one of my children who is having a hard time in school – and then there's the friend with no job – and then there's the Middle East situation – etc.

Do you have such a list as the above? I've decided I could either worry myself to death, dreaming up various scenarios of what might or could happen for the worst. I could worry myself sick or take a sabbatical, as Jill Carr suggested.

The first thing I did was to look up the word in the dictionary just to be sure that I did this thing right. It said that sabbatical was a time of rest and worship. Gosh, doesn't that sound grand? Rest and worship! Then I took one of my Christmas presents, a wonderful blank book from Prim and proceeded to write at the top of each page the date and the word "Sabbatical." Right under the heading, I wrote "Morning Prayer;" in the middle of the page, I wrote "Bible-Reading Meditation;" and at the end of each page I wrote "Evening Prayer." There's plenty of space left between these dividers for my "To Do" list. Thus far, the pages look much like my usual days (half done), but interspersed are these grand rest and worship times, where I've written down passages of scripture or prayers that have helped me float through the day and get geared up and centered down and refilled. Do you know what I mean?

Since New Year's, I have talked to so many exhausted people. Our material secular world recommends R&R (rest and relaxation), and I do think it does help mental and physical exhaustion. But as Christians, I think we need to go farther and take sabbaticals, even if it's just for five minutes a day, for rest and worship! It not only restores the mental and physical sides of our nature, but more importantly, our spiritual side.

Brad Wilson, our Assistant Rector, once asked during a sermon if we knew which of the Ten Commandments every single one of us weekly break? I pridefully thought, "None, at least not weekly." He then said the fourth commandment, "Remember the Sabbath and keep it Holy." And he was right, for originally the Sabbath was on Saturdays, but as Christians, we worship and rest on Sundays, not Saturdays. It was kind of a trick question, but it has still stuck with me, for do we really keep a Sabbath day or any set-apart sabbatical time? It's a gift from God, you know, starting right at the beginning with His Creation and continuing not only in the Old Testament, but in the New Testament – during Jesus' life and continuing with the apostles and continuing.

I'm reading the wonderful book *Celebration of Discipline* by Richard J. Foster. On page 27 he talks about "Otium Sanctum" – holy leisure. He says the church fathers often spoke of "Otium Sanctum," holy leisure. It refers to a sense of balance in life, an ability to be at peace through the activities of the day, an ability to rest and take time to enjoy beauty, an ability to pace ourselves.

Often our Lord Jesus would go away to a lonely place and pray. I love reading about these retreats. They didn't occur on off days, when things were slowing down a little in our Lord's life, but instead, during His busiest, most demanding times – even life and death times – His own – He went alone to pray.

If our Lord Jesus Christ, the Son of our Almighty God, needed these sabbatical rest and worship times, how can we possibly think that we don't? Aren't we each trying to the best of our ability and as the Holy Spirit guides us, to live more and more like our Lord? That doesn't mean busier and busier!

Again, quoting from *Celebration*, "In contemporary society our Adversary (devil) majors in three things: noise, hurry and crowds. If he can keep us engaged in 'muchness' and 'manyness', he will rest satisfied. Psychiatrist Carl Jung once remarked, 'Hurry is not of the Devil, it is the Devil'."

As I said, I am a little apprehensive about this coming year, but to combat this apprehension, I am not going to get busier, I am going to get benched. I'm going to give myself more sofa sabbaticals. The original gift of the Sabbath was given to us by our Lord God. It will be the ultimate gift that keeps on giving, for it will "restoreth my soul" and yours, too.

Your couch potato sister in Christ,

Lucy

It's Epiphany: "A Christian festival commemorating the manifestation of Christ to the gentiles in the persons of the Magi." The Epiphany collect: "O God, who by the leading of a star didst manifest thy only begotten Son to the peoples of the earth: *Lead us, who know thee now by faith, to the presence, where we may behold thy glory face to face;* through the same Jesus Christ our Lord, who liveth and reigneth with thee and the Holy Spirit, one God, now and forever. Amen." A grand sabbatical prayer, don't you think?

Precious Group,

I'm still crying!

Thank you, Lord.

I've been on a crying binge since yesterday afternoon and it feels so good! Winton wisely counseled me to go say "Good-bye" to Grandma. So I got in my car at 4:30 p.m. and drove to Birmingham – and that's when it started – the gusher of tears. I put on wonderful praise music and sang and cried all the way home.

I use the word "home" because it was like taking a trip back in time to my beginning home – for the memories just poured in. Grandma represents to me most of my childhood and many of my aspirations and dreams. I was raised in a unique situation, at least it's becoming both unique and rare these days, for we had an old-fashioned extended family. Grandma lived with us, or rather we lived with Grandma.

You see, my grandfather died the year I was born. My mama and daddy had built a house next door. It was decided, when I was five, that we would move in with my grandmother so that she wouldn't have to move or live alone. And I'm so glad we did. It was a grand, wonderful old Colonial house with banisters that you could slide down and hidden closets that you could play in, but best of all, was the blue room where Grandma lived.

Although the door was often shut, it was never locked, and all I had to do was knock and it was opened. (That's why that scripture, **Matthew 7:7**, "Knock and it shall be opened," has always made sense to me.) And what a haven it was! I was always met with a warm greeting. I knew I was loved and welcomed. She taught me to sew. I was in charge of wrapping her Christmas presents. She'd often share an apple with me. She'd slice and serve and even today, I find that is the best way to eat Eve's fruit – with a companion. She'd take me on Sundays to St. Martins-in-the-Pines to serve tea to the old people. We'd go to Morrison's for hamburger steak.

But best of all would be the talks. There was an overstuffed chintz chair that I was allowed to sit in, preferably correctly, but often I'd sit in it with my legs hung over the arm and there we'd talk about anything. I mean, anything. She was unshockable, unprejudiced and a grand listener. She smiled and laughed and advised me all the way through my childhood years and all the way through my high school years and all the way through my college years.

Many of our life choices have paralleled, for Grandma is my step-grandmother. She married my grandfather, who was a widower with three children. I married Winton, who was a widower with three children. She married at her parents' home in their garden. I married at my parent's home in the garden. She moved from Montgomery to Birmingham. I moved from Birmingham to Montgomery. Anyway, can you tell I've been having a wonderful time reminiscing — and mourning, yes, mourning. Grandma is 94 and is failing fast. Mentally, she is sharp as a tack, but since before Christmas, she has not been able to keep any food down. The doctor says that there's really nothing that can be done, for her esophagus has worn out. So, I went to tell her good-bye — until I join her on the other side. Oh, and I thank the Dear Lord that He gave me this privilege, for I've never had this luxury before. The only other close deaths that I have experienced were sudden deaths and there was no good-bye time. Good-bye time is important and very healing and therapeutic.

All this past week, I've really enjoyed going back and reading Genesis. There are grand good-bye scenes. At the end of Abraham, Isaac and Jacob's life — each gave his blessing and each was mourned — blessings and tears, and that's what went on between Grandma and me.

I spent about an hour with her. When I walked into her room she said twice, "You came just in time," not morbidly, or sadly, just stating a fact. One reason Grandma has always been so delightful and entertaining is that she lives in the present and always has. We didn't talk about our old glorious memories, for we were still making new ones.

She wanted to know about what was going on now with my family — what the latest trend was in Montgomery — how our Christmas trip went — to please tell Winton, "Thank you," for sending her the book review on her brother's biography (Cliff Durr) — she thanked me for her Christmas sweater. She apologized for not being very "entertaining." Can you imagine? She was fighting back nausea with every breath.

I was the one that wasn't very entertaining, but that was fine, I was saying "good-bye." What do you do? Well, I just sat next to her bed and put my hand on her tiny shoulder (4'10" — 85 lbs.) and silently prayed, giving thanks to our Almighty God for this saint in my life and to please not let her suffer much longer. And to take her into His Almighty arms quickly. I read Psalms to her. She shut her eyes and listened and wiped away a tear. She continued to be the lady and the hostess, for when the night nurse came in, she introduced me.

When it was time to leave, I gave her a kiss and told her, "I love you." She said, "I believe you do." And I said, "Grandma, you have influenced me more than anyone else in my life!" Then I left, got back in my car, put the music back on and continued with praying, praising and tears, all the way to Mama's house.

Mama wasn't home and when I called Winton, neither was he. I was disappointed because I wanted to share some of the "good-bye" with them, but then I realized that it was to be between me and Grandma and that's the way it should be. (I know, here I am writing you and sharing it with the whole world – but there's been some space time – some rest and reflection time.)

When I came to get in the bed last night, on the end of the bed was a note from Mama and a present. I opened it up and much to my delight found a crèche scene for the lake. I immediately set it up on the table directly across from the bed. I took the little lamp from the bathroom to illuminate the scene – Mary and Joseph adoring the Baby. It was beautiful and was the last light I turned off before going to sleep.

And this morning, it was the first light on. The figures remind me of how good we are at saying hello. They represent the Holy Mother and Father greeting their Holy Child. We know how that's done. We've all ooohed and aaahed over meeting and greeting new babies. We've all ooohed and aaahed over meeting and greeting new and old friends. I think we've got it down pat how to say hello – it's the good-byes where we have problems. I think we have a hard time ending things, letting them wind down and come to conclusion and completion. At least, that's how it's been with me, for my world has gone so fast that I blast through life without closing doors gently behind. I think I've slammed them instead. High school – slam! Brother died – slam! College – slam! Father died –slam! Moved from Birmingham – slam! Moved from Montgomery – slam! Moved from Miami – slam! Moved from Lakeland – slam! Grandparents died – slam! Moved from Montgomery – slam! Moved from Wilmington – slam! I know with each transition I didn't exit "grace-full-ly," and behind each slammed door are a lot of good-byes that I didn't allow to happen and I believe you can't let go if you don't say good-bye.

But ah, the difference I feel about Grandma. There was no door-slamming done yesterday. We enjoyed each other immensely and shared our love and shared our good-byes and the door was gently closed. And just like the door to her blue room growing up, it wasn't locked. I can open the door at any time and visit and remember with great joy until we are together again.

Hanging above the table with the crèche is a painting which has hung there for the last 14 years. I've never really studied it before today. I used to think I didn't like it because it's painted in the blurred impressionist style. I know I must be the only one alive who doesn't love impressionism, but for me they seem just half-baked ideas – like they weren't quite "done." Anyway, this painting, this unjelled painting has grown on me this morning. It's an outdoor scene. Two figures are sitting under a tree watching a gray-haired lady and a little girl walking together. This morning, it has come to symbolize Grandma and me and our walks and our talks and our times shared. They will continue – on the other side.

I again want to thank my heavenly Father for allowing me this "grace-full" good-bye time with Grandma.

And what about those past door-slamming episodes? Well, I plan to go back in my memory and ask the Lord in prayer to help me to open some of those doors and to ask the Lord in prayer to help me shut them a little more gently and to ask the Lord in prayer, where necessary, to heal them a little more completely, so that those needed good-byes can be said "grace-full-ly" – full of His grace.

As this New Year continues to unfold, might you also be needing to go back and reopen and reclose some doors properly? Do you also have some old slammed doors that need to be shut a little more gently and "grace-full-ly," too?

Jesus said, "I am the door; if anyone enters through Me; seek and you shall find; knock and it shall be opened to you. For everyone who asks, receives, and he who seeks, finds, and to him who knocks, it shall be opened." **Matthew 7:7-8.** That sounds like He is a wonderful doorman, doesn't it?

And what if Grandma lives to the ripe old age of 100? Well, I'm so glad that we've said our good-byes, so that from now on we'll just look on our time together as gift time and with great joy.

In the movie *Little Big Man*, there was an Indian who was contrary, for he did everything backwards. He'd walk backward instead of forward and he'd say "good-bye," when he meant "hello." You know, there might have been great wisdom there, starting a relationship with good-byes might not be a bad idea. For with hello, there seems to always be some possessiveness, but with good-bye, there's a letting go and seeing the relationship more as it really is –
a gift from the Giver.

My prayer for Grandma is an old one used by Israel (**Genesis 46:30**) and Semion (**Luke 2:29**) "Lord, now lettest thou thy servant depart in peace," but if not now, we'll enjoy our gift time until the door gently closes – only to be opened again – by our Lord.

Your sister in Christ,

Lucy

Precious Group,

"Your love has lifted me higher than I've ever been lifted before."

I love to wake during the night or in the early morning hours with a song in my heart, especially if it's one of my favorite hymns or anthems. But this morning, much to my surprise and delight, a pop tune was playing in my brain. "Your love has lifted me higher than I've ever been lifted before."

I'm sure the reason for this pop rock ringing in my head is that it is the type of music being played once more in my car – WLBF has given way to WHHY. All buttons have been re-programmed to pop rock, for a teenager, Alysoun, once more reigns over my radio.

And that's OK, for I remember how important music was to my own adolescent world. On those days when you felt like you didn't have a friend – your life was going to pot – you made a "D" on a test – you had no date for the dance – you didn't have a thing to wear – your parents were nerds and didn't understand you – plus, to top everything else, a bump was coming up on your chin – there was always a perfect maudlin melody to play over and over again that exactly expressed your miserable mood.

And on the other hand – when the sun was shining and you felt pretty and popular and you were pleased not only with your social life, but even school wasn't so bad and your parents weren't getting on your case, there again was just the right record to say "everything's O.K. – at least for today."

So, in order to gauge my new lady friend's world, I let her push the buttons. And when she responds to my routine question of, "How was your day?" with the routine answer, "Fine," I then can get a more complete picture through our radio communications. If my companion slouches down in her seat and plays sad and slow tunes, I can respond one way, whereas if I have a singing go-go dancer who's being restrained only by a seat belt, I can respond differently.

Now, back to my morning melody á la Alysoun – "Your love has lifted me higher than I've ever been lifted before." Yes! Thank you, Lord! Your love has lifted me higher – and I'm so glad!

This week has been so oppressive! First, I went to Atlanta to my monthly Forum Meeting. This group consists of ten precious ladies from the Southeast. The common bond that brought us together was being married to business executives. The common bond that keeps us together is our willingness to intimately share our lives with each other. With the sharing comes great compassion and caring. A grand gift, but often a heavy load to carry. Especially this month, for it seemed that each one of us was burdened down – deep. I left the meeting with my mind and mood in the trenches. We shared – we cared – and I dug a trench.

The image that comes to mind is one of those old black and white World War II movies, where you have a battalion of men who've been bombarded for days by the enemy – so they've dug-in and they're stuck in the rut of a trench. Sure, they have the companionship of their comrades-in-arms hovering next to each other and that's some comfort. But the reality of a trench, I mean a real WW II trench reality – is that bombs keep dropping, havoc keeps happening and you just dig in deeper. There is no real future planning of digging out, you just know the present survival plan of digging deeper into that trench.

And that's the mood I found myself in as I left Atlanta. I felt like a defeated retreat was being made rather than a ride home. And then I just kept digging my trench deeper and deeper until I couldn't seem to get out. Help! Help! Do you know where I turned for help? I turned to CNN!

Now I ask you, where in all of my Biblical training did it say that when things got heavy, turn to CNN? Did I think that seeing war up close would alleviate the pain and worry? Did I think that by observing the war hour upon hour, day and night I would be helping those suffering? Sure, it did make me have empathy at first, but as I became almost addicted to the reporting, I wonder whether apathy was starting to take its place?

And then, an almost silent, inward scream of, "I can't take this any more!" and finally, thank the Dear Lord, I realized by the grace of God, that I wasn't supposed to take it. I wasn't called to get into the trenches with the troops, but instead, as a Christian, I was called to set my eyes on Jesus. Yes, in all situations – set my eyes on Jesus.

I then got out my Bible and started reading – out loud – reading. Oh, I wish I knew the Word so well that I could skip around, always pulling out the perfect verse for every problem. But no, I guess I'd be so prideful with that gift that it would never work. So where did I begin? **Matthew, Chapter 1: Verse 1** – reading out loud!

Ahhh! I could breathe again! And there was a lightness, so that I felt like I almost floated out of that trench, that self-inflicted trench.

Of course we are to care and be concerned for our fellowman, but instead of joining them in the trenches via CNN, I believe they will be better supported on the home front by our constant prayers and praise to our Lord God. For it is He who reigns – not just on blue sky days, but He reigns even more brilliantly on dark ones.

A dark scene that has really stuck close to me this week is found in **Matthew 14:22-33**.

It tells of a storm raging at sea and all the Disciples were being tossed to and fro in their little sailboat and I'm sure, were scared to death. I know that feeling because I've been sailing at Lake Martin, enjoying myself immensely, feeling confident, so confident in fact, that I sailed a little farther away from home than usual. I didn't worry, because the wind was so good and constant. I felt that I could get home quickly, if necessary. Then, all of a sudden from out of nowhere came a storm, with rain and high winds and lightning and white-capped waves. I was scared to death! I can imagine the Disciples' fright and I can imagine the relief felt as their Lord Jesus came to rescue them.

But impulsive Peter couldn't wait! He jumped out of the boat with the total assurance that he was going to join his Lord, right then and there! He was so sure of his and his Savior's relationship that he just knew he could walk on that water just like his Lord. And he could, you know, he could as long as his eyes were on Jesus. His faith made him buoyant! He was buoyant as long as his Savior and not the storm permeated his mind. His footing was sure. But once the darkness of the storm seeped back in, once again, only then did the sinking begin.

Like Peter, this week I briefly lost some of my buoyancy, for I had my eyes glued to the Gulf crisis and not to my Almighty God. And then — I read — out loud — about a storm where Jesus came and said, "Be of good cheer, it is I; be not afraid." **Matthew 14:27**.

Ahhh! I can breathe again and float, too! What are you glued to these days?

Your sister in Christ,
Lucy

Jan. 28

Precious Group,

The dog died. Dam!

What a senseless waste — so unnecessary! I'm so angry because there's not a dam thing I can do about it, at least that's the way I feel right now. Why? Lord, why? I mean cancer at 48, isn't that enough? A daughter's daddy dying — isn't that enough?

The dog ate poison. We've been asked to bury him — at least that's something we can do. When things seem senseless, we bake cakes and send flowers and huddle together and hug and cry and ask, "Why?" And say, "Dam." Of course, I know how to spell that word. It's not out of piety that I've left off the N, it's just that as I wrote, the meaning seemed more appropriate written this way. Life seems to be flowing pretty smoothly and then the sense-less happens, one of those Job jobs, and everything comes to a screeching halt — like a

500-foot dam has been instantly dropped into place. You have to deal with thoughts like, "Wait a minute, what's happening here? Life was going pretty smoothly and now 'wham!' I've hit a brick wall – dam, I mean."

Don't get me wrong. I don't believe my Lord God is a zapper. I do, however, believe that He allows evil to happen – it's part of our fallen state. And we make choices and sin does happen. And I do believe that it is by the grace of God that bad can be turned into good. I love when Joseph said to his brother, his repentant brothers, who'd sold him into slavery, "You meant it for evil; but God meant it for good." **Genesis 50:20.** That is my hope, always. I believe even the senseless will make sense – in God's time.

So today – we dig a grave for Billy the dog. Dam! The digging does seem to help, for we're at least doing something and by doing something the dam doesn't seem so formidable.

So, life goes on for now – there will be more "D days," I'm sure, for that is the reality of our fallenness.

"D days" like:

Disease ....dam!

Drugs..dam!

Divorce ....dam!

Disasters ....dam!

Death ....dam!

Depression ....dam!

And our immediate response may be "dam!" to all the above, meaning – hold it! Something big has just fallen into my path. I've got a major blockage here! Help!

You might think, "Come off it Lucy, really. I don't think you should rank a dog's death with the ones listed above. I mean, really! We've got a war going on now, girl – I mean, big time 'D days' are continually happening." And I found myself thinking that way, too. I rationalize, – there are just too many hurts to mourn. I don't have enough tears, so I'll just save them up and shed them only for the biggies. But can you imagine the hardheartedness that could occur.

And then I read this wonderful scripture: "Blessed be God, even the Father of our Lord Jesus Christ, the Father of mercies, and the God of all comfort; Who comforteth us in *all* tribulation, that we may be able to comfort them which are in any trouble, by the comfort wherewith we ourselves are comforted of God." **II Corinthians 1:3-4.**

We don't have to run our pain through the Richter scale to see if it qualifies for real tribulation, and only those measuring over a five would get God's attention. He says He'll comfort us in *all* our tribulations. That's such good news! With friends, I know I've occasionally met their pain and sorrows not with compassion, but one-upmanship: "Boy, you think you've had a bad day, let me tell you about mine!"

Thank the Dear Lord, that's not how He operates. Jesus didn't say, "Today I'll only help the ten most hurting." He said, "Come unto me, *all* ye that labor and are heavy laden and I will give you rest." That inclusive *all*! Thank you, Lord!

One more thing that I'd like to share is a new insight that our Assistant Rector gave me on the word "comfort." I called him to ask what were the comfortable Words. After responding, he then said that comfort was not meant to be a warm fuzzy, instead the word meant: com (with) + fort (strength) = with strength. Thus I conclude: The Holy Spirit is called "The Comforter" = "the Strengthener." Wow!

So, I've had a "D day," not necessarily one of the biggest "D days" in my life, but nevertheless, it was a downer and that counts in my Lord God's book, for they *all* count. And what will I do with these feelings? Well, we dug a grave and buried Billy the dog. Over his grave we placed a little St. Francis statue that had belonged to his owner's mother, Virginia Bear. She left it over eleven years ago when we bought her home. It never really had a permanent garden site before. It's been kind of the wandering yard statue all these years. But now, it's firmly fixed where it belongs. And then, we said a prayer of thanksgiving for this precious pet and then we were comforted – by the God of *all* comfort – who understands.

And what are the comfortable Words which have been a part of our Holy Communion since 1543?

Matthew 11:28: "Come unto me, all ye that labor and are heavy laden, and I will give you rest."

John 3:16: "For God so loved the world, that he gave his only begotten Son, that whosoever believeth in him should not perish, but have everlasting life."

I Timothy 1:15: "This is a faithful saying, and worthy of all acceptation, that Christ Jesus came into the world to save sinners; of whom I am chief."

John 2:1-2: "And if any man sin, we have an advocate with the Father, Jesus Christ the righteous. And he is the propitiation of our sins: and not for ours only, but also for the sins of the whole world."

Comfortable Words = Strengthening Words

By accepting His strength given through His Word...

By accepting His strength given by the Holy Spirit…

By accepting His strength given by my Lord and Savior's life and death and resurrection…

By accepting His strength given by the saints that have gone before…

By accepting His strength given by friends, through hugs and pansies to plant on Billy the dog's grave.

I have been comforted. Thank you, Lord. May you now use me more to comfort others. May I no longer meet friends' "D days" with one-upmanship, but with a heart full of hugs from You, the Comforter = the Strengthener. Precious group — I thank the Lord for you and your hugs.

Love,

Lucy

Feb. 10

Precious Group,

All present and accounted for — the patient, the father, the girlfriend and the godmother. We were all crowded into a tiny little cubicle. In fact, we took up all the available seating space so that when the doctor arrived, he had to stand during the whole inquisition. And it truly was like The Inquisition, for we drilled the physician with every conceivable question concerning chemotherapy and its known side effects.

We were all united in purpose, which was to go through this entire ordeal with Carl as much as was humanly possible. I would like to emphasize the "humanly possible" aspect of this walking side-by-side with a friend who's going through a life trauma. This united intent has never been more beautifully expressed than by Ruth to Naomi, "Entreat me not to leave thee, or to return from following after thee: for whither thou goest, I will go; and where thou lodgest, I will lodge: thy people shall be my people, and thy God my God: Where thou diest, will I die, and there will I be buried: the Lord do so to me, and more also, if aught but death part thee and me." **Ruth 1:16-17**.

As I said, we wanted to be present with Carl as much as was humanly possible — but the reality was that "present" for us meant whenever it was convenient or whenever our own daily agendas allowed.

I don't mean to be cynical, for we were and are totally sincere in our commitment to this brother in Christ — again, its just that we're human and thus limited in our capacity to be present with one another.

But the good news – the unbelievable good news – is that we have a God who is omni-present, present everywhere at once. And thank the Dear Lord, all week long I've been reminded and comforted by this reality.

First, at the Women's Prayer Retreat last Saturday, we ended our day with organized worship. It was "organized" in that in preparation, we were divided into four groups and each assigned an aspect of God's character to represent. We were to find two scriptures to read and a hymn to sing during the service which declared that characteristic. My group was assigned "Omnipresence." The scriptures we selected were:

Psalm 139:7-12

7   Whither shall I go from thy Spirit? Or whither shall I flee from thy presence?

8   If I ascend up into heaven, thou art there: if I make my bed in hell, behold, thou art there.

9   If I take the wings of the morning, and swell in the uttermost parts of the sea;

10 Even there shall thy hand lead me, and thy right hand shall hold me.

11 If I say, Surely the darkness shall cover me, even the night shall be light about me.

12 Yea, the darkness hideth not from thee; but the night shineth as the day: the darkness and the light are both alike to thee.

and

Romans 8:38-39

38 For I am persuaded, that neither death, nor life, nor angels, nor principalities, nor powers, nor things present, nor things to come,

39 Nor height, nor depth, nor any other creature, shall be able to separate us from the love of God, which is in Christ Jesus our Lord.

and best of all, Jesus' last words in the Gospel of **Matthew 28:20**: "Lo, I am with you always, even unto the end of the world."

Just reading them always allows me to breathe a sigh of relief! "Yes, Lord. It's OK, Lord. I can breathe again, Lord!" Especially this week, I often unexpectedly found myself shallow breathing. I found myself becoming stifled by chemo and car pools and commitments. I would be panting because I was trying to be present more than was humanly possible. Then I'd recall the Saturday Worship Service of praise and acknowledging our God's omnipotence = all powerful and our God's omniscience = all knowing and our God's omnipresence = all present, allowing me to breathe deeply again.

And thank the Dear Lord, I received a mid-week refresher course at our 5:30 Informal Worship Service. Our minister prayed:

"Father, come into our limited minds, fill us with Your omnipresence. Come into our weak hearts and fill us with Your omnipotence. Come into our lack of faith and fill us with Your omniscience as to all the wonderful things You can do. To those and through those we call upon the name of Your Son, our Lord Jesus Christ. In Your Holy Spirit be with us and speak to us now. Amen!"

I know that it was because of these constant reminders that I was made more keenly aware of my Lord God's omnipresence all week long. I know that it was because of this aware-ness that instead of being rushed out of breath, I experienced the most profound peace that I've ever experienced in my whole life. Of course, I've had moments before, but never days.

This week should have been unbearable and would have been unbearable if I'd have tried to do it alone – a new class starting, plus two flower arranging classes to teach, plus walking with a friend through treatment, plus the usual – but His calm peace prevailed. That's one of the grand by-products of acknowledging His Presence – peace – profound peace. I wish I could capture it in words – I can't – but I can quote:

Philippians 4:7: "And the peace of God, which passeth all understanding, shall keep your hearts and minds through Christ Jesus."

Isaiah 26:3: "Thou wilt keep him in perfect peace, whose mind is stayed on thee: because he trusteth in thee."

John 14:27: "Peace I leave with you, my peace I give unto you: not as the world giveth, give I unto you. Let not your heart be troubled, neither let it be afraid."

And I can leave you with a birthday party report. Friday was my dear friend Madeliene's birthday. It also was the anniversary date of my father's death. I see our friendship, Mad's and mine, as an unexpected gift from the Lord. We became friends while working on our church's Bizarre Bazaar. When I found out her birthday date, I experienced an inward smile. This "hole" day – a day which had been a "loss" day, because of missing my daddy, had become a "whole" day again by being my friend's birthday.

Well, anyway, to celebrate this awesome occasion, we had a "spend-the-night-party" at the lake – me, Mad, and Carol (another God-gift). We had cheese whiz and daiquiris and frozen entrees for our celebration. I know it doesn't sound too appetizing or dietetic, but it was easy on the preparation and clean up time and that was of the utmost importance! We wanted to relish this rare time together and relinquish all KP duty to Daisy the dog, who can lick any aluminum container spotless!

We were all exhausted for we'd all been experiencing numerous heavy days, weeks and months – but we were determined to stay up and enjoy each other for as long as possible. But at last, we gave in and went to bed. I was less reluctant than the others because I knew the best was yet to come, for the surprise present would be arriving in the morning.

And sure enough, she did: it was "Mary Barwick with Slides." Mary pointed out that some birthdays feature clowns or magicians. We were most fortunate, for we had Mary and she was grand! We went to the back room, closed all the curtains, put up the movie screen, sat on the floor and ate popcorn as Mary read to us her latest unpublished book. We learned what "The Alabama Angels" were currently up to. I won't spoil the surprise for you. I will, however, tell you that those angels will mightily remind you of the Lord God's omnipresence and the by-product of His peace will be so strong that you'll have to take the day off, as we did.

For after the story with slides, all we could do was just walk together on the beach, sit in the sun together, and eat lunch together. We were like slugs – no, snails – no, saints. We were like saints, I think, for this wonderful togetherness we have with our Lord God, or omnipresent Lord God.

Peace – profound peace – Holy peace – rolled in on us that birthday and it still lingers on. Saints act out of that awareness, don't you think?

Masha shared with me "My Psalm #1" by Melanie Morris written at "Lake Lucy" in March of last year at that year's prayer Retreat. The peace continues:

My Psalm #1

"As surely as the wind
is whispering thru these
pines – and lapping
at these waters – so
too your Spirit whispers
thru my heart strings
and laps at the still
waters of my soul.

As surely as the
warmth of sunshine
filters thru these
pines – so too the
warmth of your love
filters thru the shade
of life's trials, and
warms my heart.

Oh, the peace of it all
– the gift of peace from you.
It is no wonder that
we are drawn to these waters –
it is no wonder that we
are even more
drawn to the Living
Water that is You,
Oh Lord!"

Oh, I forgot to tell you the hymn we chose for the Saturday service – "Surely the Presence of the Lord is in this place. I can feel His mighty power and His grace…."

Peace – Friends! We're saints because of our togetherness with Him!

Your sister in Christ,

Lucy

Feb. 26

Precious Group,

"Beautiful" just woke me up. It's 4:00 o'clock in the morning and I'm so very tired, for we had a late night of it. It first started with fixing supper, then serving supper, then cleaning up after supper (good girl Lucy, you should do that more often!) – then the night continued with television viewing, homework supervising, book reading, and then finally bed, at least for the first time.

Then the alarm went off, the visual alarm that I have been trained to perceive over the years – it's the green telephone light which indicates a conversation is in progress. I don't know why it is, but I can be sound asleep with a pillow over my head and then "bing" – the silent alarm goes off in my brain. A chain reaction instantly occurs. I look to the right, see the light, pop out of bed to go chop off a head! I know it doesn't sound very compassionate and it isn't – it's just become an inbred reaction from raising four teenagers.

When they were little, I had that same reaction of popping out of bed when I'd hear just one weak "Mom" called out. It always amazed me that the decibel frequency of that one word could only be heard by a mother. Have you also noticed that at your house? You have this big, beautiful hunk of a husband sleeping next to you who becomes deaf in the dark and dumb when he dreams, but regresses to a boy who remembers that Moms do the midnight watch.

You know what? I bet those big old guys in their beds not only become little boys, but aren't even asleep after all! They probably are just pretending like we used to pretend that we were asleep on Christmas Eve. We'd wait up in bed with our eyes shut, waiting for Santa to come. I bet those big old husbands wait up in bed with their eyes shut to be sure that Moms still come when called.

And I did, frequently and with compassion. But somewhere down the time-line, the children grew and the night calls changed into the night callers, and my compassion went when the green light of the phone came on. Consoling Mom changed into the Phone Crone. My soothing night voice changed into one of a shrilling shrew. "It's past your bedtime. Get off that phone," would be my battle cry.

And that's what I was aiming to say to Alysoun as I took the stairs two at a time last night at 10:30. I had only one mission to accomplish, which was to extinguish the green light – whatever the cost. I burst into the room, ready to attack the excuses. I was prepared for any and all of them. I knew my years of active duty would serve me well. My speech was prepared: "Young lady, don't you know what time it is?"

But instead of being met with excuses, I was met with a crying child – one crying her heart out and the Mom compassion of old had to kick in to the godmother. I had to relinquish my Enforcer of the Night role and opt for someone else to take control. I left her on the phone, alone, with a friend. I sat in the hall and allowed her to continue the conversation for 30 more minutes. I guess I'm an old softy, but I was so glad that this precious child was getting all this junk out. She'd complained of having a headache earlier and now I knew it was from

holding all these "uckys" in and I was glad she was having an explosion instead of an implosion, and allowing all these feelings out.

My prayer in the hall was for the friend on the phone to be a compassionate counselor and consoler – one who would and could listen and allow Alysoun to lean on her for the moment, while she unloaded her pain and worries and insecurities. And I think the friend was, for I could mainly hear (not eavesdropping, but sound surveillance) Alysoun sobbing and talking, with little time for the friend to respond and that was perfect.

I knew, for I'd received the same treatment earlier that day. I had silently sobbed in sentences, not tears, to a friend. She listened and counseled and served coffee. Thank you, Lord, for compassionate Christian friends – there's nothing like them!

Sometimes I try to close my eyes and envision my Lord Jesus' face, but I can't. I sometimes can visualize His pierced feet and sometimes I can even imagine kissing them and anointing them with oil. Sometimes I can envision His arms giving me a hug. But where I've really felt like I've seen Him, or such a strong resemblance that I know I will be able to recognize Him when we meet Face to face, is in the eyes of a compassionate friend. Those accepting eyes have enveloped my soul and His calm peace has rolled in like a gentle mist, bathing and refreshing my spirit – like a whiff of "Beautiful."

It was this Esteé Lauder smell which woke me up this morning and it's a pleasant way to arise. I must have turned over and smelled my hand which had earlier hugged Alysoun. You see, she wears "Beautiful," which is a perfect scent for her. And, violà! Her perfume brought me out of unconsciousness into His consciousness that "everything is going to be all right" – for we have a Friend, a Compassionate Friend.

I looked up the word "compassionate" in *Webster's* and it said, "sympathetic consciousness of others' distress together with a desire to alleviate it."

And then I looked up the word "compassion" in the Bible as it referred to our Lord. And here are just a few of the passages:

Matthew 9:36: "He was moved with *compassion*…."

Matthew 15:32: "I have *compassion* on the multitude…."

Matthew 20:34: "So Jesus had *compassion* on them…."

Mark 1:41: "And Jesus, moved with *compassion*…."

Mark 5:19: (The Lord) "…hath had *compassion* on thee."

Luke 7:13: "When the Lord saw her, he had *compassion* on her…."

Luke 10:33: "He had *compassion* on him…."

There is no question in my mind that one of our Lord Jesus' attributes was and is and always will be – compassion. It was through His working out of this compassionate nature that we have His infinite compassion expressed through His Passion.

I read or heard that the world received no bigger embrace than when Jesus' arms were stretched out on the cross and I believe in that one blessed, beautitudinal act – the Compassionate Friend embraced us all.

This morning, I was awakened by a whiff of "Beautiful" and yesterday I inwardly sobbed in sentences to a friend who served coffee and listened compassionately. Then, we went to see the brand new baby lambs at my father-in-law's, which reminded me of a verse (don't worry, I had to look it up) **Matthew 9:36**: "But when he saw the multitudes, he was moved with compassion on them, because they fainted and were scattered abroad, as sheep having no shepherd." It is because of His compassionate nature that He became the Shepherd and I don't have to go around frantic like those mother ewes I saw yesterday. I don't have to go around frantic or frightened or in a frenzy ever again and neither do you, because we do have a Shepherd who is a constant, compassionate Companion.

Yesterday, I was reminded of this glorious reality by getting just a little whiff of coffee and cologne. They were a grand aromatic blend which helped me through the day and night. They were a grand pick-me-up – no caffeine, no calories, no cholesterol, just a reminder of our Companion – you know, the constant, compassionate One. Rejoice people! We are not alone! Alleluia and Amen!

I pray for you daily and give thanks for you. The Lord has a mighty army when His compassionate Christian friends gather in His name – may His troops continue to gather and multiply!

Your sister in Christ,
Lucy

Precious Group,

The cards that stole my heart as an eight-year-old, broke my heart as a forty-two-year-old. Lord, may it stay broken.

Thursday, Madeliene and I met my Mama and sister for lunch at the lake. It was grand. We sat out on the dock and drank hot cider. It felt like we were on some grand ocean liner, with the wind blowing and we were wrapped up on deck. The good news was that we had already reached our desired destination — the lake.

It was only a short visit, but we still had time enough to soak up the tranquil beauty. I believe I could sit on that dock for eternity — just sit and watch nature do its dance. The ever-changing clouds and water and sun and moon and stars. Oh, it's grand and balancing. All is well, always, after a stay on the dock. It doesn't matter what season or time of day — the result is always the same — deep peace.

We then came in and shared a delicious lunch. Mama told me she'd brought a little surprise for me. While cleaning out drawers, she had come across an old scrapbook of mine and brought it to me. It was brown leather and had "Scrapbook" written in gold. It looked vaguely familiar. I knew it had been mine and I assumed it had to have been of high school vintage, for that was the memento age, as I recalled.

I opened the yellowed pages up and much to my surprise and delight, the treasures of an eight-year-old unfolded before my eyes. It had valentines scotchtaped to the pages and a telegram from my favorite teacher, Miss Robinson, and a letter from my grandfather's seventy-year-old cousin, who I knew had loved me. Each little memento seemed to blow silent kisses to me from the past.

And then I came to two cards, one sent from Los Angeles and one sent from New York City, and it was those two postcards of old that broke my heart. They were both addressed to "Darling Lucy" and one of them said "Don't forget your Uncle Chris." And that was the statement that started the "heart crack" — for you see, I had.

I had forgotten, or at least had forgotten the Uncle Chris as seen by an innocent eight-year-old. Grand memories began to flood back into my mind. I remembered when Uncle Chris would come home, it was like a celebrity had arrived. We children would put on plays for him. Everything seemed a little enchanted. He never stayed long, always brought gifts, and played the piano and told about his exotic travels and told about the latest play or song that he'd written. At eight, I thought him a handsome adventurer. As an adult, I viewed him more as a lost soul.

The thing that hit home so hard was the innocence lost, my innocence. At some point along the way, my eight-year-old innocent, accepting and yes, loving eyes had been replaced by jaded, judging ones. And with judgement, came hardness of heart. The older I got and the more mature I became (whatever that means), I began to glean from my own observations, plus others, that Uncle Chris wasn't so glamorous after all. None of the plays and songs were ever hits. None of the jobs he held were for very long. He died at age 59. Tragic, I used to think. What a waste, I used to think. What missed opportunities, I used to think.

But then this week, I saw the postcards and with those postcards come the pain and the realization that I'd become an accomplished judge, using my standards, not Jesus'. Lord, forgive. I realized that there were a whole lot of "Uncle Chris's" in my life — those just not quite living up to my standards. Lord, forgive. The real tragedy, I realized, was that innocent, accepting love had given way to limited, conditional, judging love. Lord, forgive.

I saw the postcards and a crack was felt in my heart. I hope and pray that the crack continues until my heart is totally broken so that innocence once more can reappear. Innocence is defined as "uncorrupted by evil, malice, or wrong-doing; sinless; untainted; pure."

Jesus said, "Suffer the little children to come unto me, for such is the kingdom of heaven." I believe it was the innocence and acceptance and love that our Lord was pointing out to those people gathered, those mature, got-it-together people, so "gotten together" that they were jaded and hard-hearted and crackless. Notice, I didn't say flawless, but crackless and hard-hearted.

But how can we remain innocent as children all through our lives? Is that possible? I believe only at places like Father Purcell's Exceptional Center; maybe that's why it is called exceptional. These children are extremely handicapped, both mentally and physically. Somehow this reality seems to have placed them into an innocence time capsule. It is a place of love and acceptance and celebration of the little things — a smile, a wave, or a sound becomes a monumental moment. To feel the softness of a sixteen-year-old's hand that had never been polluted by the hardships of life is to hold a dove in your hand. To look into eyes of total innocence is to get a glimpse of the heavenlys. That's why I feel most comfortable playing with the children on my knees. The awe — generated by innocence — is awesome.

But for us who are out in the *real* world, the polluted world, the "sin full" world, how do we keep that innocence that our Lord Jesus Christ delighted in? How do we keep our hearts pliable and growing with the love of Jesus, as opposed to hard-hearted and shrinking from sin?

I believe it is only by His grace and by keeping our eyes continually on Him. I believe it is only by His grace and by being in constant prayer and supplication. I believe it is only by His grace and by remembering always what our almighty God did for each one of us, remembering that the Love Incarnate came down and hung on a cross, so that each one of us might be in a personal relationship with Him. Wow! Isn't that awesome and humbling? Doesn't that just crack and break pride and self-righteous judgement and hearts?

Joel 2:13a says, "Rend your heart, and not your garments and turn unto the Lord your God."

The Psalmist says, "The Lord is nigh (near) unto them that are of a broken heart…." **Psalm 34:18.** And, "The sacrifices of God are broken spirit: a broken and a contrite heart, O God, thou wilt not despise." **Psalm 51:17.**

And in **Luke,** the first time that Jesus claimed His Messiahship, it says, "He found the place where it was written 'The Spirit of the Lord is upon me, because he hath anointed me to preach the gospel to the poor; he hath sent me to heal the broken-hearted, to preach deliverance to the captive, and recovering of sight to the blind, to set at liberty them that are bruised. To preach the acceptable year of the Lord!' And he closed the book and he gave it again to the minister and sat down. And the eyes of all were fastened on him. And he began to say unto them, 'This day is this scripture fulfilled in your ears.'" **Luke 4:18-21.**

I bet when Jesus finished talking, you didn't hear a pin drop, but hearts cracking and breaking. And thanks be to God, His Word continues to crack us and carrying our tailor-made crosses continues to crack us — and receiving a card once more from Uncle Chris — well, you know what it did — crack!

Thank you, Lord! Break us and make us into Your Image!

Love, Your Sister in Christ,
Lucy

March 6, 1991

P.S. After Morning Prayer, I asked Masha to critique this letter before I gave it to you. Winton was unavailable, for he had to leave for work at 6:00 a.m. Masha is my friend and fellow volunteer at Father Purcell's and a daily Morning Prayer partner. She has a gentle spirit and is a gift. I handed her this letter. She handed me this poem:

Innocence By Masha

Eyes lit up with inexpressible thought
Somewhere inside little spirits are caught

Poor fragile bodies, they sit in their chairs
Patiently waiting, accepting our care.

We bring them music and try to hold hands,
One gentle touch they do understand.

We really don't know the world where they are
They might see angels or rainbows or stars.

A smile on its way will sometimes break out,
Or sound that is quite a wonderful shout.

Children forever but God loves them all—
More blessed than we, in sin they can't fall.

LL

St. Croix, Virgin Islands
Holy Week

Precious Group,

Today are you a participator or a possum player? In other words, today are you a do-er or a be-er?

I must confess that all week long I've been the latter instead of the former and I continue to be. Right now I'm sitting on the beach in a wonderfully protected, tented blue cabana. It's like a double bed with a half tester on the top. I can expose myself to the elements as much or as little as I want. I'm protected, which is preferable when you're just be-ing, for you're more vulnerable in this state. You tend to absorb your surroundings as opposed to react to them. And right now, that's all I want to do, for I've got to sit on the sidelines of life for a little while until I finish processing the deaths of Charlie and Tim. They were two children that lived at Father Purcell's Exceptional Center. Both had lived there almost all of their twelve years of life and both had died there within the past week. I'd known them only in the capacity of being their weekly volunteer music lady. In all the years, I'd never really gotten Charlie to respond in any noticeable manner. His blue, blue eyes seemed already focused on another world. Tim, however, I knew loved earthly music, especially classical.

The rest of our party of eight is learning to scuba in the ocean. For the last hour they've been swimming and kicking and carrying on while I've been observing like a hermit crab under my blue tent. Maybe I've really been more like a soft-shell crab, for I seem to have shed my protective covering. My hard shell has had to come off, for I've experienced a new pivotal point in my life and with pivotal points you must shed your old-shelled self so you can grow. And a growth opportunity is what Charlie and Tim gave me. During their lives I gave them volunteer hours, but at their death, they gave me the pivotal point of rock solid blessed assurance. At this moment:

I must stop the world and say, "Thank you."

I must pause for a brief intermission and say, "Thank you."

I must play taps in my mind for these two precious children of God, who yelled out to me at death, "Peace."

Thank you, boys.

It's now dusk and another day. I'm looking out of our bedroom window. There seems to have descended on this entire world a translucent veil which gives everything a gossamer glow. Thank goodness for this softening of the extremes, for the extremes of wind and sun and heat can be oppressive. Barbara, my friend and fellow mom on this trip shared with me her insight that we are more lovers of the lake than of the beach because we enjoy moderation more than extreme. Give me a gentle breeze over a pounding wind any day. Give me sunscreen number four and a humid eighty degrees over sunblock number fifteen and a blistering ninety degrees any day.

The relief of the haze is welcomed. It seems to act as a transitional curtain between the departing day and the arriving night. I can no longer see the pounding sun, for it has set. The ocean seems to have settled down a bit, along with the wind. Everything feels more moderate and somehow, more balanced. Thank you, Lord.

The gentler breeze reminds me of the blowing fan at Father Purcell's and I must go back…. Last Friday I arrived at our usual time, 9:30, and the head nurse said that Charlie had died 30 minutes earlier and would I like to see the body? I thought how heartless the word "body" was, but then later I realized how appropriate. I had never seen new death, I'd only seen processed death. "Lucy Blount – gross!" Well, it is gross! Death with makeup is not a pretty picture, but death with white linen sheets and little stuffed animals on the bed and a cloth rolled up under the chin to keep the mouth closed was right – was how it's been handled for ages and correctly so. It was a holy death.

Love   Mary Barwick

I was left alone in the room. You could feel a calm serenity and peace clinging to the air. A fan was gently blowing like a continual breath. And then, four days later, another death. I visited once more, out of respect and homage. Neither visit felt like a good-bye, but rather a release.

I look with joyful anticipation at seeing these two precious babies again on the other side. I might not recognize them at first, for they and I will be "whole" as never before, but then there will come grand smiles of recognition. I'll finally learn what Charlie's blue, blue eyes were looking at for all these past years and Tim will tell me which melody he really liked best. They'll get to say thank you for the music time, but best of all, and most importantly, I'll get to say thank you for their blessed assurance given.

Because of their shared departures – I know that I know that I know that I know that I know – even deeper. Of course, I've known for as long as I can remember that Jesus is my Lord and my Rock and my Savior in whom I put my trust. I've known and I know, but as I said, the knowledge is now deeper.

Just as this gossamer glow of dusk separates the day from the night, I saw in Charlie's and Tim's departures their days turned into a dawning, the ultimate dawning. I could have sworn that the angels were still hovering close, but all I could see or feel or hear was a little fan blowing its gentle breeze, reminding me of the "Ultimate Breath," my Lord God's.

It's been a very interesting Holy Week, one entirely different from last year's. As you may recall in those earlier Passion Week letters, I was a total participator, or so I thought. If the church doors opened, I was there morning, noon and night. I was fervently writing and record- ing every monumental or minuscule thought or feeling I had. I felt like I had a front-row seat.

This year I've been more on the sidelines and I think that's OK, in fact, possibly better. I've been processing instead of participating. I've been processing the boys' deaths and, I believe, processing to a deeper degree our Lord Jesus' death.

This week I was a stranger at two churches in St. Croix: St. Paul's on Palm Sunday and Holy Cross on Good Friday. It was at Holy Cross that I was allowed to go deeper. I was the only non-native. During the service the priest walked to the rear of the church where I was seated and handed me his prayer book. I felt it was a silent declaration of, "Welcome, sister sojourner!" I was no longer a stranger.

His homilies given during the three-hour service were based on the collects for Holy Week. He personalized Christ's pain, shame, loss, scourging, suffering, betrayal, death. I was surrounded by men, women and children whose ancestors, only a little over a century ago, had been slaves in the fields outside this church's walls; the same church walls had been devastated by Hurricane Hugo. They were Resurrection People. The walls had been rebuilt. Their ancestors' shackles had been broken. "Holy Cross" was a good name, for only through the cross can we have redemption; only through the cross can we be truly free; only through the cross can devastation be turned into a declaration of faith.

At Holy Cross they made this pilgrim feel no longer a stranger, but a sister sojourner and I thank them for this welcome. It profoundly reminds me of the "Welcome Happy Morning" to come – Christ's – Tim's – Charlie's – yours – mine.

"Blessed Assurance." Again, thank you, boys. At your departures you reminded me of our Ultimate Dawning.

> Because of Jesus, I am your sister sojourner,
> Lucy

Jesus said to Jairus, a father of a twelve-year-old child who had died, "Fear not: believe only, and she shall be made whole." And then He said, "Weep not; she is not dead, but sleepeth." And then He said, "'Maid, arise.' And her spirit came again, and she arose straightway…." **Luke 8:50, 52, 54-55**.

Ode of a Soft-Shell Crab

Here's to the St. Croix party of eight
who allows me not to participate.

While you snorkel and scuba and swim and sun,
I am a bump on a log and really no fun.

You want to parasail and shop and explore;
I want to get in a fetal position and be a bore.

You want to dine, dance and play games,
to go meet the new neighbors and find out their names.

I want to hide. You want to seek.
I want to stay in my valley. You want to reach peaks.

There's no telling why you're putting up with me,
and I want to say "thank you" for just letting me "be."

Don't worry. Don't hurry. Don't doubt the outcome.
Lucy hasn't had a lobotomy, nor have I gone dumb.

It's just, you see, I need a rest
to process experiences I have to digest.

If I don't slow down and take things in,
but keep running and running and running to blend

into this crazy, hazy, fast world of ours,
where "busyness" is the monster that devours

peace and calm and meditation and prayer,
solitude occasionally, where the music doesn't blare.

I need this space. I need this time.
I need a safe haven where I can "be" with the Divine.

There's so much happening in this glorious world;
why, right before my very eyes miracles do unfurl.

Little ones, big ones, all shapes and sizes,
there's no limit in the "glory" that daily arises.

No limits, except those put on by modern man
and I am as guilty as the next, if I don't notice the fan.

The fan, the fan which mentally keeps blowing,
keeps planting a seed which is ready for growing,

growing in order to crack my old shell,
to expand my horizons in the world in which I dwell.

The crack comes. The growth does occur,
because you allow me to "be" with the "Big Sir."

My Lord, my God, gently leads me deeper.
He knows I am a simple child and really a slow creeper.

He allows me to be who I am and to go at my own speed;
a stiff-necked, wavering, wandering child He continually
    does lead.

He leads, I follow more or less depending on my mood,
no team player here – by right He should have sued.

But no, His way is gentle – Fatherly – and kind.
He says, "This way, child, you're getting a little behind."

Behind, but not forgotten – no, He always keeps on
    calling:
"Yoo hoo, this way, child of mine, and can you do a little
    less falling?"

"But Father, in my fallen state I do some of my best
    growing.
On bended knees, humility reigns and that awful pride
    stops showing."

So here I sit, under my blue tent, waiting on the beach,
like a soft-shell crab with no defense, but easily He can
    teach.

"Teach me, Lord, I beg of You, the truths you'd have me
    learn.
I'm willing to grow a little bit now and take in what you'd
    have me discern."

Then I'll put my armored shell back on and continue in the
    battle,
The size might be a little large and possibly I'll rattle.

But I know you'll continually walk with me while I grow to
    the right size,
and when it's time to shed once more, I'm sure you will
    advise.

So ready or not, here I come, back into the world I go.
Thanks, group, for letting me "be" and now may I join the
    show?

For the show must go on as it always does and that's
    the way it should be,
but if you feel a call to have a great fall, please feel
    perfectly free…

Just to "be" with Him.

Precious Group,

Mary could have said, "No!" and stopped the flow – the flow of God's grace. Lord, forgive.

Lord, forgive. How often have I said, "No!" …said, "I don't feel like it!" …said "I'll do it later!" …but never did. Lord, forgive.

Lord, forgive me for those innumerable times when I've ignored those inward nudges, those gently nagging pulls which You have so graciously sent my way. Often You've silently called, "This way, child," and I've responded with a "No, Lord!" Oh, maybe I haven't been that blatant with my rebellion. My approach was more subtle. I would just turn up the volume on the Christian radio station or become busier in my do-good projects. Nevertheless, I knew and my Lord God knew that my response was a resounding, road blocking, "No!" Lord, forgive.

Why, did you know that one little insignificant-looking two-letter word can stop God's grace dead in its tracks? Oh, don't get me wrong, I'm not so powerful and neither are you. It's just with this free will gift given by our Lord God, He allows us to make choices. We can make right ones. We can make wrong ones. We can make surrendering "Yes" ones and thus be empowered by His Holy Spirit, or we can make stubborn, stuck "No" ones and try to wing it ourselves.

Often, I've made the latter choice and inevitably had to crash-land, but with each fall, my Lord God has met me, lovingly brushed me off and set me back on my feet. I know our life journey is supposed to be a straight and narrow one. If, however, you tried to map out the routes I've taken, it would look more like a maze than a fine line. Why, I've slammed into more roadblocks and dead ends! I've made more wrong turns because of my "No, Lord" lingo. Lord, forgive.

Maybe you can relate. And what's even more disgusting is that we do discuss the mistakes over and over again. We replay the wrong turns. Now, talk about going nowhere and a real downer. Why, there's nothing worse! We ask for our Lord God's forgiveness. He gives it, puts us back on the right track and then we have the audacity to "Play it again, Sam." Oh, how tiring and non-productive.

Speaking of wrong turns, why only last week I went on a wonderful, whirlwind car trip to Eureka Springs, Arkansas, to see the Passion Play — twelve hours going — twelve hours returning, all in a three-day time-span. My two dearest friends and I made our first Annual Pilgrimage. We see our friendship as a God-gift and have vowed to yearly take time from our busy schedules for a celebration of this gift. We feel this has become an imperative, for one of the group is moving. We don't know where our yearly jaunts will take us and it really doesn't matter as long as it meets our one criteria: God-centered. God-centered so that it will help us to refocus or re-align or just remind us of His Lordship in our lives.

Well, back to the trip. What tickled and amazed me was that my two cohorts love to drive. I don't. So, for the whole required 24 hours of driving, they took turns either being navigator or driver. Now, this was just fine with me. I would occasionally offer to relieve them, just to be courteous, but needless to say, the answer was, "No. We'd never get there!" They were perceptive, for my sense of direction is nil and my driving speed is usually slow. So, I'd again relax on the back seat and watch my A-type controllers do their thing — while I just went along for the ride and would sing. It was delightful.

What astounded and amazed me was that these two ladies got us to our destination in record time and instead of rejoicing that we hadn't ended up in Opp, Alabama, instead of Eureka Springs, Arkansas, they discussed for two days a little detour that they had not anticipated. They rehashed the highway numbers and the longitudinal and latitudinal directions. This seemed very important to figure out how they'd gone wrong. I wanted to say,

"Hold it girls! We're here! Forget the bad turn. That's old news. You did a grand job. You got us to our desired destination. That required a celebration, not a castigation." But instead I looked perplexed too, like, "What are we to do? We arrived, but how did we arrive? Oh dear! Oh dear!" (I'm no dummy and I knew that I needed to join in the chagrin.)

And isn't that just like our human nature? I'm sure if we are fortunate enough to ever hear, "Well done, good, and faithful servant," we'll probably say, "But wait just a minute, please, let me dig up some old dirt to wallow in, let me show You some old rags that haven't been washed, let me get out some old garbage that still smells." Why is it? Why is it that it's so hard for us to accept His grace, that free-flowing grace which comes with that one little word, yes — "Yes, Lord."

We're good at replaying the garbage, but not so good at retelling the grace flows. I don't know why, but somehow it's easier to rehash the negative than it is to relive the right-on-track episodes. But Hear ye! Hear ye! That's what we're called to do. It says that we are to dwell on "whatever is true, whatever is honorable, whatever is right, whatever is pure, whatever is lively, whatever is good repute, if there is any excellence and if worthy of praise, let your mind dwell on these things." **Philippians 4:8**.

That's what keeps us on track. That's what will help with the amplification of our Lord's call. That's what will make the reception of our hearts clearer. Yes, it is a still, small voice which becomes even clearer in the cacophony of this world if we just listen and learn.

A good Old Testament story of getting stuck is found in **Genesis 19:26**. Lot's wife turned into a salt pillar because she looked back, probably yearningly looked back, mentally retracing her old world tracks, whereas Lot and the rest of his family were forwardly marching, following their Father's lead. She became stuck as stone. The rest claimed new ground. It's all in the choices made.

And then there's the modern day Mary and the cards. It happened just last week. We met to supposedly sign a contract and that we did, but more importantly we met for coffee and a hug and a re-telling of an adventure — a grace-filled adventure which we had shared and also want to share with you.

Our conversation started with Mary quietly saying, "Lucy, do you realize how close I came to saying 'No'? That's the scary reality." But the good news is that she didn't and that's what needs to be documented, for it was a grand and glorious grace flow.

The operative words were, of course, "Yes, Lord. Yes."

Love,

Lucy

Precious Group,

"Lighten up, Lucy! You're taking yourself too seriously! Relax in the Lord! Your world is pretty rosy. Your children are healthy. Your husband has a job. You have a roof over your head. I mean really, you better be walking in joy, for life doesn't get much better! What's the big deal?"

This was the pep talk that I gave to myself all week long. On the outside everything looked pretty much like smooth sailing, but on the inside, I'd been "inner plaiting." You know "inner plaiting." It's when you take three strands of responsibility and you start mentally braiding them. As the week progressed, or rather digressed, the braid got woven tighter and tighter until I thought I might scream. The braid was becoming knotted and gnarled, for there was no joy in my activity. The martyr syndrome was setting in, but I couldn't understand what actually was the problem. I felt pulled to the left – pulled to the right – go team – go team – fight – fight – fight.

As I write this cheer, I realize that "lean" is the correct active verb, not "pulled." Oh! What an enlightening mistake. It was my attitude toward the required activities that was the problem. When you lean toward something, you're already in an attitude of going forward. It can be an attitude of humble submission, surrender by choice – a "go with the flow" mentality as opposed to a stiff-necked pull.

There is not a more poignant picture of leaning into a situation than our Lord Jesus carrying His own cross down the Via Dolorosa to calvary. I've always been deeply moved by dramatic representations of this scene. I've felt that the bleeding back of our Lord Jesus was bent from this burden carried, and rightly so, but today I realize that more important than His "burden bend" was our Christ's "loving lean" forward into the reality of His death and dying for us. I bet when Simon of Cyrene took the physical load from His back, He still continued to lean into the reality – kept seizing the opportunity – kept surrendering into the crucifixion with every step forward.

And here I am dragging my feet as if they were rock-laden. I don't want to do any of my checklist. The responsibilities are heavy laden because of my attitude. Let's see if we can get to the root of the problem. The bottom line is:

I don't want to be responsible.

I don't want to be

I don't want to

I don't want

I don't

I

There lies the problem! Lord, forgive.

(Continued a month later…)

You can't lean when you're "I" oriented, for it is the most stuck position there is. A real deep freeze of the heart occurs. There is no room for growth. There is no room for caring. There is no room for love – His or ours.

And then I think of the beloved disciple, John, and how it says on the night of the Last Supper he leaned on our Lord's shoulder. Wouldn't you love to be known as the disciple who leaned on the Lord? Totally leaned? I don't believe this position John took was just a one-night occurrence, for the Bible repeatedly uses the phrase when describing him. I believe he leaned all the rest of this life. Oh, wouldn't that be grand and glorious to be known as such?

To be able to lean, we must be flexible, with a good root system, just as our Lord described in the parable of the seed. A few weeks ago I received a deeper understanding of this truth. I drove to Birmingham for a meeting. I had heard about the horrendous storms they had recently experienced and I knew there had been great damage done, but little did I realize the extent of that damage. We see documented disasters on the TV, but they remain somehow contained in the tube and are thus easily forgotten. But to physically drive through devastation and experience it first-hand is not so easy to capsulate.

Everywhere I looked there were these huge old trees snapped in two as if a giant had taken a stroll, whereas the smaller trees and bushes were still standing as if nothing had occurred. I learned from a horticulturist that the survivors were those who could bend and be flexible and had a deep root system. Those big, old, puffed-up "I" trees broke in the storm, whereas the little leaning ones did just fine.

We can learn from this example. We need a deep root system too, one that can hold with the loads that life affords. We need to lean on Jesus, just like John did and just like all the other saints and disciples have. Our Lord's shoulders are plenty wide enough for us all. We just have to be willing to let our vertical "I's" lean a little forward into submission and surrender.

Psalm 61:1-2

"Hear my cry, O God; attend unto my prayer.
From the end of the earth will I cry unto thee,
when my heart is overwhelmed: lead me
to the rock that is higher than I."

"lead me to the rock that is higher than I"

"lead me to the rock that is higher "

"lead me to the rock"

"lead me"

Do you notice what has disappeared when we get to the basics? That's right? That awful "I." To Him be the glory!

Your sister in Christ,

Leaning Lucy

May 28

Precious Group,

Peace. I'm at Lake Martin. It's 6:00 in the morning and I'm sitting outside on the balcony. It's located at the top of the house, tree-top level and adjacent to the "Fill My Cup Chaplet." Don't you just love that name?

It was christened thus two weeks ago. While driving home from Lake Burton, Georgia, after attending a Women's Retreat, my friend Baba and I happened upon this bazaar-looking store. It was aptly named "Up the Creek." We instantly knew that it was our kind of place, because on the porch was a purple rocking chair. You see, designer clothes have never made us covet, but purple paint, however, is an entirely different story. It's not the color that snaps the trap, but rather, the attitude it represents.

We wanted to meet the person who woke up one morning and said, "Yes, I know what I can do with great aunt Sally's ugly chair. Paint it purple."

The whole store was filled with such jewels. Soda cans had been turned into airplanes and flatware had become eyeglasses. To top it off, the owner said that all of her artists were local Christians. She said that she demanded that they be drug-free and she only kept 10% commission. "Oh, how noble," we thought and we purchased with pleasure, knowing that we were helping all those Georgian saints survive.

Finally we made it back to the car loaded down with our goods. We had barely enough room to maneuver. We bought a five-foot bench painted like a watermelon and an angel Gabriel hooked rug, which just happened to have been completed the day before by an 87-year-old Georgian saint. We bought a wooden church steeple, a pair of flatware eyeglasses and a walking cane made in the shape of a cross. It was crafted by a 19-year-old boy whom everyone thought was mentally retarded, but, "Praise the Lord," wasn't. Last but not least, we

Joy

Mary Barwick

purchased a bird feeder made in the shape of a church. It was covered in buttons and broken glass and had a china tea set glued to its roof. Voilà – the "Fill My Cup Bird House."

It was love at first sight. I knew this item not only belonged in the chaplet (a diminutive chapel), but more importantly, the chaplet needs to be its namesake. You see, "Fill my cup, Lord," was often the prayer prayed and answered in the room at the top.

Now, back to the Georgia journey. After we'd gotten about a mile down the road, we started giggling. We realized that we had probably been sold a bill of goods at the "Up the Creek" store. We wondered if the saleslady had seen the crosses around our necks and decided to use the old poor, pitiful Christian artist routine.

We then started hysterically laughing and proceeded to produce appropriate sales-pitch scripts for Buddhists, Moslems, and Jews. We figure that she possibly had rolled-up prayer rugs and incense burners and stars of David in a closet and would choose the proper prop for each customer. It was fun to pretend and fun to giggle, of course all in jest. It lightened the oppression that had unknowingly seeped into our souls. For the past three days, nine of us had shared our life stories and some of them had been weighty and burdensome like the heavy cloud cover that has silently rolled in while I've been writing you.

The early morning sunrise has now been covered by clouds, thick menacing clouds, oppressive clouds. All month long the weather has been like this. Instead of the usual four inches of rain, we've had 12 inches. I'm beginning to feel like I'm molding. I feel like I can't deep breathe when there's such a continuous cloud cover as we've been experiencing. Last night, Winton called on the phone and asked if everything looked lush. "No!" I thought. To me every plant looked limp like it wanted to say, "I can't take another drop of this stuff! Please, Lord, bring in a little drought or dehydration. Let this blessed dampness depart," – and ditto for me!

This grey sky month has matched perfectly with the roller-coaster emotions I've been experiencing – up, down, all around. May always is good-bye time, a completion time, a commencement time. You have to gear up – to get ready to say good-bye. Gosh, it's awful. You work, work, work – plan and prepare and perform and then it's over. And do you know what has been getting me through this loop-the-loop of emotions? Laughter and side-splitting giggles.

I had never realized before how closely kin tears and laughter are. I think they're two sides of the same coin. It wasn't that I was hysterical all month long, but when the Chicken Little Sky Falling syndrome would kick in, it was laughter that would lighten the load. That uncontrollable giggle-type laughter would change my mental state of zero visibility into one where the sky was the limit.

For example: "9000 Christmas cards arrive next Thursday," was the refrain I repeated every five minutes last week at a luncheon. My mother, sister and sister-in-law were present. They tried to carry on normal conversations as I would rudely interrupt — "9000 Christmas cards arrive next Thursday." Not having received any measurable response, I then proceeded to simultaneously giggle and cry. Actually, I guess you'd say hysteria set in. These loving ladies instantly stopped eating and turned to me with great dismay. I could see their concern and the unspoken thought of, "Oh dear, Lucy's lost it!"

But no, I hadn't. In fact, I'd actually regained "it." My giggles and tears had broken through the burden barrier that I had been busily building during lunch. The air cleared and I could breathe once more. My mental ceiling was no longer at zero visibility. Oh, I still didn't know and don't know today how I'm going to sell 9000 Christmas cards, but the laughter helped me to lighten up a lot and allowed the Lord to rightly regain His Lordship over the situation.

And then there was the doom and gloom of having to say good-bye to a best friend who's moving. All month long we've been slowly saying good-bye. It's been kind of a spiralling down, a slow heart-tear and not a clean rip at all. Last Wednesday was especially painful. It's our church's informal worship and praise service. It's a small intimate gathering where over the years fellow sisters and brothers in Christ have truly shared their life stories. There's always joy in the worship, humility in the prayers and truthfulness in the testimonies. There are no masks worn on Wednesday nights. With this in mind, the reality was (as Mary Barwick would say), we were down. Judy, Carol and I were in a grieving mode at supper — that was, until uncontrollable laughter broke out. It resulted from the retelling of a hilarious incident (semi X-rated and thus censored). The laughter was wonderful — refreshing — a real gift of grace. The heaviness once again was lifted.

And then on my birthday, which was last Saturday, I attended a funeral of a dear friend's mother. Of course, this wasn't how I had expected to celebrate my 43rd birthday, but it wasn't a bad way at all; in fact, it was a blessing. "Sick, Lucy!" you might think, but no, it really was grand. Four friends drove to Anniston in a Noah-type deluge. It took two hours up and two hours back and it rained the entire time. We got soaked to the bone walking to the church. We got soaked to the bone walking to the cemetery. We got soaked to the bone walking to lunch. Thank goodness I had on a drip-dry dress.

Once again, it was laughter that lifted our spirits. Judy and I got the giggles during the service. We had both unconsciously been accompanying the organist by humming the hymns.

In fact, at one time we got so carried away that we started humming in harmony. I leaned over and whispered, "They will think Montgomery brought a kazoo choir." Well, the giggles started and the silent shaking of shoulders followed. I'm sure most people thought we were uncontrollably crying and had no idea that we were dealing with a giggle gusher.

There was no disrespect intended or, I believe, incurred. Our response actually went well with our surroundings. The name of the church was Grace Church and it was appropriately named, for it was grace-filled. The window over the altar was of Jesus pointing to a field of lilies. It was so realistic that you could shut your eyes and almost hear Him say, "Consider the lilies of the field...." And when He spoke those words initially, I bet grace flowed and giggles gurgled just as Judy and I experienced. He probably was surrounded by a horde of people who felt that his or her individual world was uniquely oppressive. Each of them probably carried a burden which was so heavy that each felt that there was no hope for his or her situation. And then – the Lord said, "Consider the lilies of the field...." What an energizing breath of fresh air must have been taken. What a rejuvenation of spirit must have transpired, just like the one Judy and I experienced. The cloud covers in their minds started lifting and then I bet contagious, joyful laughter started reverberating throughout the crowd, just as Judy and I experienced.

Grace. How does one respond to this wonderful gift? With humility and thanksgiving and praise – and occasionally an appropriate laugh.

In **Genesis 18:12** it says that, "Sarah laughed."

In my twenties I thought: How embarrassing! Sarah made such a fool of herself. She laughed at such an inopportune time. God Almighty visited her home. At first, she responded rather appropriately by preparing a delicious meal. Then she lost her composure. She hid. She eavesdropped. She learned that through grace she was to be a post-menstrual mother. She then giggled. "How gauche!" I thought. We're dealing here with a mature woman, not an ingenue. Why, Sarah was well-traveled, frequently entertained and was responsible for the running of a rather large household. Surely she had more sophistication and sense of presence than that!

In my thirties I thought: Now I can better understand poor Sarah. She was just a product of her time. Her inappropriate behavior was fostered by a male-dominated culture. She was probably insecure and lacked equal educational opportunities. Women's lib hadn't hit her world yet. I spoke with great authority because I'd traveled to Saudi Arabia and experienced first-hand this 'Sarah-type situation.' I had sat on the floor and eaten with men, while the women were kept behind closed doors. I could imagine Sarah being with them, still hiding and eavesdropping and giggling. But I thought, surely she had more sophistication and sense of presence than that!

In my forties – to be more specific, on my 43rd birthday – I finally understood the reason for Sarah's laughter. It had to do with grace. You see, the Lord spoke. Her barrenness was to be turned into fruitfulness. Her misery was to be transformed by a miracle – a grace-full miracle. How does one respond? Often, at first, with a laugh or giggle. Sarah did have a "sense of presence," a sense of our Lord God's presence. And to make room for the bigness of the Reality, often a spontaneous laugh occurs.

Peace – from the top of the "Fill My Cup Chaplet" – at Lake Martin, Alabama. And if by chance you start feeling a giggle attack coming on, be sure and relax and enjoy it. It has nothing to do with sophistication – but a sense of presence – our Lord God's presence.

With love,
Lucy

June 11

Precious Group,

Believe it or not, I'm learning how to click and drag and point on a computer. You must understand that the likelihood of my acquiring these new skills has been nil, for my lifelong war cry for years has been, "Never!" Once again I find myself having to eat crow. In fact, I'm learning that this diet of having to eat my words is a healthy one, for the growth that takes place is in the mind, rather than in the middle.

Winton and I are in Boca Grand, Florida, for three days. The assigned activity for the trip is tarpon fishing, but the real reason is to celebrate and to keep current our twenty-plus years friendship with the Hirons. The good news is that with such a relationship everyone is so relaxed that even assigned activities can be altered, if so desired.

For example, it's our last day and I haven't gone fishing yet and still don't plan to go and that's OK. Of course, such rudeness would not have been tolerated fifteen or twenty years ago. Attending scheduled activities was then mandatory. Luckily, today the story is different. The men go fishing while Marty and I play on her computer. Computer! What a joke! Me on a computer!

It still hasn't sunk in that I can learn this skill. Winton aptly captured the essence of this erroneous fit when, after returning from his first day's outing, said, "I'll be less surprised at the second coming than my surprise at finding you on a computer!" I just meekly smiled and continued on with my Apple program. You see, this poor man has tried for years to get me interested in this machine. He'd promoted it at conferences and meetings whenever introductory classes have been offered. He's even ordered one because of some package deal.

He'd try to convince me with, "Lucy, just think of what you can do! You can put your recipes on it, and make a list of all the people who attend our parties, so there's no overlapping of menus." Well, needless to say, this neither excited me nor sold me on the need. Thus far, my few party menus fit quite nicely on 3' x 5' cards, and thank goodness friends attend for fellowship, not variety of fare. In fact, I've gotten it down to a science. If it's Wednesday, you get vegetable soup. If it's Friday, you get tuna. If it's Saturday, you have the luxury of two choices – steak or "Chicken Lucy." Winton has named this poultry dish not for my originality (both Mama's of course), but because it's the usual.

So, computers and I haven't mixed thus far; that is until Monday when Marty gave me my first lesson. I must give her, and not the machine the credit for making it user friendly. Let me share with you some of Marty's tips. ("I" is used for ownership, ours over the computer, not vice versa.)

1. "I" only use it to do what "I" want it to do.
2. "I" take one step at a time.
3. "I" don't want to know anymore than "I" have to know for the specific job I'm doing.
4. Don't tell me how it works, just tell me what it takes to do what "I" want it to do. I'm too old to learn any more than that.
5. Don't ask why, ask how.
6. "I" know "I" can do it if I take the time to learn. "I" have the ability. It's the time that's the problem.
7. To learn these new skills, I'm going to have to say "No" to some other activities. I can't be fractured. I must block out time needed to perfect the skill.
8. All of it is very simple. It just takes time to learn.
9. Lucy, you can do this!

I think what freed me up so that I will be able eventually to operate in this new field is the reality that "I *can*" do it rather than "you *must*" do it. Somehow or another, if you say or infer or assign a "you must" activity to me, chances are you'll get a no show instead of a production. In order for me to do an activity, I have to take ownership of it. I have to choose to change the debilitating command of "you must do" into a freeing agreement of "I can do" or

"I will do." It's an attitudinal thing. If I feel like I'm being done in or duped, a red flag instantly goes up. My system shuts down as if it automatically knows this isn't the way it's designed to operate. If, however, I feel like I'm getting a choice in the matter, then I'll often take on the task. Why, I've even been known to occasionally wash a dirty dish or two. It just depends on how the task is presented.

Of course, Jesus understood this scenario. He understood the Godly gift of free-will choosing which His Father gave to each and everyone of us. He knew to handle it with great respect, for He knew that we were the only created creatures to have this freedom. Jesus demanded each and every person He encountered to make choices for him or herself. Jesus didn't give the blind beggar, Bartimaus, a debilitating handout or a set of "must do" interactions to follow. No! Instead, He said, "What do you want Me to do for you?" **Luke 18:35-43**. His question was both plain and precise. He neither infringed on Bartimaus's personhood nor took away Bartimaus's responsibility for his own actions. Our Lord offered Bartimaus, along with all the others who experienced Him, a hand up, not a hand-out. As His disciples, that should also be our rule of thumb, for that's the way we're designed to work best.

Now, if you don't mind, I'd like to bring up an old letter which has never been sent or shared because I didn't know actually what to do with it. Now, after having completed the above letter, plus having completed the computer introductory course, I think I've found the solution. See if you don't agree with its eventual surmise.

Precious Group,

I've been trying to "cookie cut" my cousin. Lord, forgive.

Conditional love? No. I won't go that far. I love her and I miss her and I think she knows this. I do need to humbly confess that I've wanted terribly to change her — change her more to my liking. Lord, forgive.

After mentally reconstructing my cousin, over the years I've moved right on to friends, and foes and family members. I realize that if I don't stop this dissecting charade, the next thing I know, my Lord Jesus will come under my hatchet.

I know this is not a pretty picture. It's even harder for me to write. Can you even imagine the possibilities? The heinous sin of my even coming close to cookie-cutting Christ — redesigning Him more to my liking, to be more user friendly, scares me to death! Lord, forgive.

The reality is that if I can do it to one of my sisters or brothers, then why not to another until, like the domino effect, I've knocked down everyone except the One and Only. And then, when it's just us two standing, me and my Lord God, He'll ask, "Lucy, what have you been doing? Where are all your fellow brothers and sisters that I've sent your way? Why have you been knocking them down instead of lifting them up and bringing them to Me?"

And I'll have to answer, "Lord, I've been trying to fix everybody and everything for you."

"But Lucy, that's My job. Remember, I'm the Creator. *I'm the One* who called each one of these precious people into being. They're Mine and I love them. *I'm the One* who sacrificed My Son, My only Son, so that I could be in communion once more with my human sheep. *I'm the One* who sent My holy Spirit to indwell the believers and to empower them. *I'm the One* who has done all this and I don't need you to fix things, for that's My department. I need you to love, not judge, not only Me, but also My children."

Gulp! "Lord, forgive."

All of a sudden I realize that over the years I've been trying to be the Creator. I've gotten into the awful habit of trying to recreate. Can you believe my audacity, my out-of-balance — and now my shame? I really believe that in some situations I've tried to be the butcher, the baker and the candlestick maker, all rolled up in one and I'd tell you what to be and what to do if you just gave me half a chance.

This has been a gradual decline to slime. Over the years family and friends have had to put up with Lucy's late night lectures. If you kept me up past my bedtime (9:00 p.m.), chances were that I'd become the problem-solving sage, self-appointed I must add. If you asked for my opinion on any subject or situation, you'd not only have gotten what you asked for, but much, much more. That's why I'm probably now allowed to go to sleep, even on Saturday nights, for who wants to be recreated and rerouted by Lucy?

Lord, forgive.

I now know that Lucy can't fix a life, only the Lord Jesus Christ can. I now know that the only thing Lucy can do is to choose to love or to judge a person. Loving seems to lighten another person's load, whereas judging seems to make the loads of life even heavier. The only person who can alleviate a load is the person carrying it. It's his or her choice. A well-known statement which has come out of the AA tradition is, "Let go. Let God." It's a simple truth, as most truths are. The relinquishing of a burden, whether a stuck situation or a personal sin, is an individual's choice which only an individual can make. That's how God made us and expects us to work. "Let go. Let God." It's a universal truth, one which I desperately needed to hear, heed, and embrace.

Back to Boca…

Now, if you don't mind, I'm going to turn on the computer, type in "Lucy, the Problem-Solving Sage" on a folder and then with my mouse, drag this file to the trash icon and throw it away so that once and for all this old crone will be canned. I no longer want to be a problem solver, but rather a lover who allows you to do your own thing and follow the path which you choose to take. If you ask, the Lord will lead you and if I ask, the Lord will lead me, but again, it's our choice to follow or not.

> Your sister in Christ,
> Lucy

And P.S. to D.D.:

I love you. I'm sorry for any pain that I've inflicted over the years, either directly or indirectly. If you see or feel or hear judgement rearing its ugly head once more, just say, "Can it, Lucy!" and I'll mentally take the mouse and drag it to my trash icon in the computer of my brain and stuff it once more. Please be patient. It'll take a little time to re-program me.

The saying goes, "You can't teach an old dog new tricks." Luckily you're not dealing with an old canine but rather a middle-aged ewe – who does love you. More importantly we're both loved by a Love who called each one of us into existence just for the sheer joy of wanting to have a relationship with each of us.

I'm sorry I've been trying to choreograph your life dance as well as mine and a whole host of others. But the good news is this self-appointed dance master has been canned, so that maybe our individual waltzes with our Lord may continue more grace-full-ly.

> LL

And P.S. to the Precious:

When I awoke this morning, I vividly recalled portions of a dream, which was highly unusual for me. As the day has evolved, the dream has evaporated. I am now left with only an image of a face. It is beautiful. It's as if it was a bronze bas-relief of my Lord Jesus' face. It is very similar to various artists' representations I've seen of Veronica's Veil. In some traditions it is believed that as Jesus carried His cross to Calvary, a woman named Veronica lovingly wiped our Lord's face with her veil or handkerchief. An image of His countenance remained imprinted on her cloth. Such was the face I saw except it seemed more bronze and shining and alive. There was one tear falling from His right eye and I knew I'd put it there. "Lord, forgive." Judgement is not my job, loving is.

What's your job description?

> LL

Precious Group, Let's Go Lighter

Little Children of the Precious Group,

Once upon a time long before there were computer games or Barbie Dolls or Ninja Turtles, there was born to a Mama and a Daddy who loved each other very much, probably much like your own parents, a tiny baby girl.

Now the Lord God had already blessed this family with a blue-eyed, blond daughter named Mary, who was now seven, and then a blue-eyed, blond son named Bill, who was now five. But this new baby would be different. For her daddy had been praying and praying that the Lord God might bless them once more with a healthy, happy child and if it wasn't too much trouble, he sure would like a baby girl with big brown eyes and shiny brown hair, just like his very own.

Well, you know nothing is impossible for our Lord God, for He makes everything and He knows and hears all of our prayers. You do know that every birthday is a special day and that the angels clap their hands with joy with each new baby born and send down a guardian angel especially assigned to help that child through life, and that's really why we celebrate birthdays.

Anyway, back to this spring day, the Lord God had been listening to Daddy Billy, who was a good man, and the Lord God knew that this little family was very sad and hurting because the children's granddaddy, Daddy Billy's father, had just died and was living once again with the angels.

The day finally arrived, and not a moment too soon (especially for Mama Beverley) and sure enough, she had a baby girl, and guess what? The baby had big brown eyes and shiny brown hair.

They named this precious child Lucy, after her grandmother, and that was a grand name for the baby to have, for the grandmother was a good and saintly lady and would be someone for their child to try to be just like.

Do you know who you were named for? I bet it was for somebody really special, like a great aunt or a great uncle or a great grandparent that your mama and daddy loved and admired. You be sure and ask them if you don't already know, for names are very important and a very special gift; in fact, the very first gift given to each one of us by our parents.

But first let me tell you a special secret. Did you know that each tiny little baby who comes into the world already has a name? That's right. The Lord God has already taken care of that from the very beginning of time and it's the very same name for each one of us. And that's what our story is all about.

We're going to follow little baby Lucy's life for a while, because I think her story will help you discover what our special secret name is. Now, I know you might be thinking, "The same name? We all have the same name? That's silly! How can we all have the same name and if we do, then how can we know who's calling whom?" Well, the answer will come soon enough, as answers always do.

Well, as I said, baby Lucy with the big brown eyes was born and they took her home from the hospital and everyone was so excited — the mother, the daddy, the sister, the brother, the grandparents, the aunts, the uncles, the cousins, the neighbors, why even the pet dog, Ricky, seemed to be a little more frisky.

And do you know the name that kept popping up? "**Precious**." And I must tell you that that's a pretty good first clue to help us learn our secret name, for "precious" is very similar to it. So, lets look a little closer at that word. Have you noticed that every time you're around a baby, I mean any baby, the grown-ups are always saying, "Isn't she just precious?" or "Isn't he just precious?" So what does precious mean?

Well, in the dictionary, it says that precious means "of great value, greatly cherished, dear." Let me see if I can give you an example. Do you have a best friend who's always fun to be with, whether you're playing together or spending the night together? You even know that if you two have a little fuss, it's OK, because you always forgive and makeup. Why, you wouldn't trade that friend for anything. Well, the way you feel about that friend is what precious is all about and that's how grown-ups feel about their babies and most brothers and sisters do too, at least as long as the baby stays in its baby bed and leaves their stuff alone.

So, the first clue to the secret name is "precious." That's not the right answer yet, it's just our first clue, but if we can find out all the clues, then we can figure out the real secret name. And we do know that Lucy's secret name is our secret name, too, for as I said, it belongs to everyone.

Lucy grew and grew, as all babies do. First, she started crawling and then she started walking and then she started talking and by three, she could even run pretty fast, but of course, not half as fast as her older sister and brother. But still, she could get around pretty well on her own.

People also started calling Lucy "cute," just because she was into everything, which of course, drove her brother and sister crazy. (Some days they didn't think she was precious or cute at all, but instead, a real pest.) She was happy and funny and giggly and just like a beam of sunshine. Ah ha! Remember that! **"Beam of sunshine"** or **"sunbeam,"** for that's another clue.

"Sunbeam," is a name that applies to every single preschooler under the sun, for have you ever tried to watch a three- or four-year-old? Why, they are so full of energy, just like the sun. If you watch younger children, you'll notice how they really are like sunbeams bouncing around, fast as lightning until they collapse and go to sleep.

So, before we go any further with Lucy's life, remember we now have two clues.

Lucy, what's your name?

Precious Sunbeam

That's right!

Now we can be off again with little Lucy. While we were talking, she continued to grow and grow. She not only grew on the outside, but she also grew on the inside, too! You know how meat and vegetables and fruits and milk help make your body grow big and strong on the outside. Why, I know you've even held up your arm and said, "feel my muscle" and you knew it was good and strong because of all those vegetables and healthy foods you've been eating.

But do you know what makes you grow big and strong on the inside? Hugs and kisses and kindness and love make you grow strong on the inside. It's from that warm loving that you've been getting while you've been growing up from parents and teachers and relatives and friends – all the special people that the Lord God allows in your life. You know, those special people that make you feel all safe and warm and peaceful inside when you're with them, like they're giving you a big hug, even though they might not be touching you. They can give you a special smile (one made just for you) – or they can give you a special pat on the back (one made just for you) – or they can give you a special hug (one made just for you) – or they can give you a special kiss (one made just for you). It's all of these "specials" given by extra-special people that you love best and that love you best that help you grow up inside and that's very important. I'd even say it's more important than those big old muscles on the outside.

Let me see if I can explain it a little more clearly. You see, in the very beginning, I mean, beginning beginning, the Bible tells how the Lord God made us and has been loving us for thousands and thousands of years. It says that in the very beginning the Lord God made us in " His Own Image." Do you know what God's image is? I mean, if God looks in a big huge mirror, do you know what He would see? "Love." That's right. "Love." But what does "Love" look like? We know what love feels like, we've already talked about that – but how does "Love" look? That's a little harder to imagine.

And God knows that, too, because He knows everything. That's why He sent His only Son, Jesus, to earth so that we could know all about "Love" by looking at Him and learning all about Him and how He lived, but even more importantly, how He died and rose again just for us. But that's another story. What is very important for each of us to remember is that if each one of us is "made in the Image of God," that means that each one of us has a "spark," or "sunbeam" of God's Love. And that's what we want to grow inside of us, even more than muscles, because that's what God is like – "Love."

But goodness gracious, how can we get love to grow? I mean that sounds very hard, doesn't it? Let's look back at little Lucy and see if she can help us.

It looks like she did everything normally. She went to kindergarten and then to grammar school and then to junior high and then to high school and then to college. She then got married and had children and now is waiting to have grandchildren.

She's had a lot of fun along the way and some sadness. You know sadness is part of life and some things hurt really bad, but she always had a feeling of a "hug in the heart," which was all the stored up love that kept her going and will keep you going too.

Now we're getting very close to knowing the secret name. We've learned that "precious" and "sunbeam" were clues and now let's add "**Love**" with a capital "L." It's a precious sunbeam of God's Love that I'm talking about. Each and every one of us has that, because as we said before, God is Love and remember that we are made in His Image, so that means we have that Love, His Love, in us. Wow!

So let's ask our question. "Lucy, what's your name (and our name, too)?"

"Precious. Sunbeam. Love."

The last two clues will be faster because they came to Lucy just this year, and they're very fresh in her mind.

First, this past Christmas the most wonderful present was from a friend. It was a pair of white plastic earrings. They looked just like buttons with some gold glitter glued on them. Lucy thought they were special, but didn't know how special until about two weeks after Christmas. She saw her friend, who told her that the glittering gold symbol said "I Love You" in sign language. And that touched Lucy's heart. (Sign language, you know, is the way people who can't hear can talk to each other.)

That present reminded her that she was precious, just like you are precious. It reminded her that she had a sunbeam of God in her, who is "Love," but best of all, it reminded her that God Almighty loved her – and He loves you too!

Peace   Mary Barwick

"I Love You," the Lord God our Creator, has been saying to us from day one. "I Love You" – all our life He's been saying to us, "I Love You." When we've been hurting and when we've been happy, He's been saying, "I Love You." When we've been running or walking or sleeping or talking – He's been saying, "I Love You." We might not always be hearing it or understanding it like our Lucy, who didn't understand what the earrings said until her friend told her. And that's OK, for remember that the Lord God is "Love" and He doesn't change and He'll keep on saying it all your whole life long – "I Love You." You'll hear it – trust me.

But what's our secret name? It took a long time for Lucy to find out, I mean most of her 42 years. And she'd been looking and trying and doing everything she could to discover it.

And then one day a letter came in the mail from a friend (thank goodness for friends, they are some of God's best messengers). The letter was addressed to: "Dear Lucy Light-bearer." "That's it!" she said, **"Light-bearer**!" That's it! That's the secret name of each and every one of us!

But what's a Light-bearer? Oh, that's the most wonderful name under the sun! So wonderful that, of course, it has to be a secret. Let me see if I can try to explain it to you so you'll understand why it's so grand and wonderful and secret.

Let's see. Have you ever been in your house at night time and there was a huge storm outside, with lightning and thunder and wind and rain and all of a sudden the lights went off? Gosh, it was really dark and scary – but then you heard your Mama or Daddy's voice and they said, "Wait just a minute. Everything is going to be all right. Let me light a match and then I'll light a candle and then we'll go from room to room and light candles all over the house so, the darkness will go away." And sure enough, the candles shining in every room made them seem warm and safe-feeling again. Well, you can call your Mama or Daddy a "Light-bearer," for "to bear" means to carry and he or she acted as "light bearers" when they went from room to room with their candles.

And that's what we all are, Light-bearers with a capital "L," for the Light we are to carry is our Lord God's. And remember, I promised at the very beginning of our story that no one would get their secret name mixed up with anyone else's, even though the name was the same for all of us. That's because each one of us has received God's loving Light differently, so each one of us gives His Light off differently. We are all to shine, like our God's created stars in the night, but each of us twinkles differently.

Of course, you do know that the Light comes from God. It's turned on in our hearts when we start hearing, "I Love You, I Love You, I Love You," that He continually says to each one of us. When we start hearing it, it hugs our heart so much that His Light just starts shining through every one of us. And it's our job to pass it on so that everyone we meet can know about our Lord God and His Love. We are to be His **Light-bearers**. And it all started a very long time ago – when God made man in "His Own Image" – Love.

So, my precious Light-bearer, now you know the secret. Guard it well, but it's important to pass it on. And the best way, as we've learned, is by giving a special smile, a special pat on the back, a special hug, or a special kiss to help remind others that our Lord God is always saying, "I Love You." That starts the light shining in someone else's heart.

Remember, precious child, to keep growing on the inside, for that's far more important than the growing on the outside!

Love – "**Light-bearer**" – Love

Like God loves you—

Always

Now, for the last time, "Lucy, what's your name (and my name, too)?"

"**Light-bearer**," precious child, "**Light-bearer**."

Many people who have read the manuscript have sent letters to Lucy.
Here are a few of their comments:

"Your letters are so wonderful and so uplifting. I love the way you take everyday life experiences and see God in them. How refreshing and encouraging."   Nan Hobbs

"You have a gift – writing, of course – but especially making one realize that 'God Is.' Too many times I forget that He is at the center of everything."   Barnett Wood

"I have just finished reading your book. The best thing I can think to say is 'Whee'."   Betty Vaughan

"Your deep faith and devotion to our Lord are expressed in such a charming and delightful fashion with such sincerity and truth that all your readers will be uplifted by these. Thank you! Thank you!"   Beverley Furniss

"Her description of nature and her surroundings as it relates to attitudes and events is remarkable."   Bolling "Bo" P. Starke, Jr.

"They are beautifully composed and they touch one's heart. You have a wonderful gift of imagery and you have a deeply creative facility that is extraordinary."   Jean Waters

"I couldn't put it down! I laughed and I cried. It grabbed all of my emotions. I think you are an incredible lady, so full of life, so full of Christ."   Rexanne White

"I could identify with so much of what you said and I would laugh so – they are uplifting."   Dorothy Christian

"Your writing is so fresh and uplifting with a special genuine tenderness."   Baba Hendricks

"I brought it home, put the children to bed (at bedtime) and could not put it down. It is beautiful – so pure – so comprehensive – so simple – yet – so deep."   Ann Thorington

"Each letter touched me just where the Lord was trying to show me something that needed a little boost or a little readjusting!"   Pat Dunn

"Lucy, I was raised Baptist and studied the Bible since 'Sunbeam Band.' In my home we read the Bible every day. In college I studied theology, so my life has been full of the Bible, but you gave me so many new and exciting concepts of its passages. I felt it was a whole new book. ...Thank you for my most exciting experience."   Muriel Hornsby

"You have launched an original vessel which will be causing ripples, waves and white caps in the lives of others forever more."   Mots Rainer

"It made me laugh, cry, think, rejoice, reminisce, praise God and be totally grateful to you for sharing it with us."   Pat Williamson